THE NON-USER-FRIENDLY
GUIDE FOR ASPIRING
TV WRITERS

THE NON-USER-FRIENDLY GUIDE FOR ASPIRING TV WRITERS

EXPERIENCE AND ADVICE FROM THE TRENCHES

Steven L. Sears

WordFire Press
Colorado Springs, Colorado

THE NON-USER-FRIENDLY GUIDE FOR ASPIRING TV WRITERS

Copyright © 2014 Steven L. Sears

ISBN: 978-1-61475-236-3

Cover design by Janet McDonald

Art Director Kevin J. Anderson

Cover artwork images by Steven L. Sears

Book Design by RuneWright, LLC
www.RuneWright.com

Published by
WordFire Press, an imprint of
WordFire, Inc.
PO Box 1840
Monument CO 80132

Kevin J. Anderson & Rebecca Moesta, Publishers

WordFire Press Trade Paperback Edition October, 2014
Printed in the USA
wordfirepress.com

DEDICATION

Dedicated to:

Burt Pearl

THE MILLION DOLLAR WRITING SERIES

When seeking advice, always consider the source. Many self-appointed "experts" write how-to books without themselves ever accomplishing the thing they are trying to teach you how to do.

In the Million Dollar Writing Series, each of our authors has sold a minimum of one million dollars of commercial product in their field. They have proved themselves, and here they share their wisdom, advice, and experience with you.

There are many factors in becoming a successful writer, and we cannot guarantee that you'll break into the top levels, but we hope you find the advice to be useful and enlightening.

CONTENTS

PREFACE

The TV industry isn't a very user-friendly business. Oh, they're very friendly and personable, and I've met with countless warm welcomes at pitch sessions and working lunches, but it's almost impossible to figure out. I've published over 125 novels with more than fifty bestsellers ... but I haven't been able to figure out TV yet.

Steven L. Sears has. We've crossed paths at countless pop-culture and media conventions where we were both guest speakers (me to talk about my Star Wars novels, Steven to talk about his work on Xena: Warrior Princess). We've been friends for twenty years—quite close friends, actually.

Because we got along so well, we naturally decided to try working on something together, and I came out to LA to stay with him while we developed a few pitches to take to the networks. But I realized that I knew little about the industry itself, all those secret handshakes and decoder rings. (It turned out that just *watching TV* did not give all the qualifications to *write for TV*.) It was going to take a career to learn all the things that I needed to know … and fortunately, Steve had spent his career working on countless television shows as a writer, producer, show runner, and series creator. You know the shows: *The A-Team*, *Riptide*, *Hardcastle and McCormick*, *Swamp Thing*, *Superboy*, *Walker-Texas Ranger*, *Xena: Warrior Princess*, *Sheena*, and so many others.

He already knew the stuff. And he had been putting together his advice, a large database of experience and knowledge, culled from his helping others online and in classes. He let me read his notes, and I found that he was able to present all that important information in an easily accessible manner. How cool was that? Like having a mentor on a stack of printouts.

I urged him to polish up all that material into a book and, despite his reluctance to become a book writer (having seen how glamorous my life as a writer is), I succeeded, and I'm very pleased with the result. And *The Non-User Friendly Guide for Aspiring TV Writers* just happens to fit perfectly into the "Million Dollar Writing Series" that my own WordFire Press is publishing. (I'm sure Steven makes a point somewhere in this book about "knowing the right people.")

In *The Non-User Friendly Guide* he shares his experience in a simple and conversational manner. It's like having lunch with Steven and asking him questions about the business. Without having to watch him eat.

Kevin J. Anderson
September, 2014

I. INTRODUCTION

This book is an experiential book. By that, I mean that you aren't going to find academic discussions on the Entertainment Industry, diagrams of story structure, or pedantic examinations of the creative process. No, this book is all about my experiences and the knowledge I have gained from them. I'm going to attempt to write it in a very accessible and friendly manner, much like I would speak if you were to just sit with me for lunch and ask questions or ask for advice. Sometimes, these might be questions that are just curiosities that occur to you, some things you don't normally hear people talk about. Or questions about the difference between the theory of the Industry and the reality of it. That's the real core of this book.

So how did this come about?

In my many years of working as a professional in the Television industry, I have had numerous people ask me questions about the business. With the expansion of the Internet, this has increased a hundredfold. Obviously, there would be many things that just kept cropping up over and over again. Not too long ago, I finally got it through my head that it would be easier to document my answers so that I wouldn't have to retype everything each time I was asked.

I soon realized that I had compiled a list of questions from these aspiring Television Writers. This list implied two things: One, these were questions that really meant something to them and, two, they weren't getting the answers anywhere else. But when I responded, I soon found out that many times they weren't always happy with the answers I gave. In some cases, they even debated whether I was telling them the truth or not.

My conclusion? I wasn't telling them what they wanted to hear; but I was telling them the truth. Good or bad, the truth isn't always what we wish it to be, but it is still the truth. Without it a person is unprepared and defenseless. I can't tell people what they want to hear; I can only tell them what they need to hear. That philosophy created this book.

In fact, though, this was never intended to be a book. I had compiled these questions and answers for a long time, but never intended to publish them. But when I decided to do it, I really thought I was onto something original. An approach that was unique. Something that would stand out. I was in a book store chatting with a friend, who was the store manager, about the possibilities of such a book. She liked it. In fact, she liked the one that was already on the shelf.

Oops.

Max Adams is an awarding winning Screenwriter who wrote "The Screenwriter's Survival Guide" and, like myself, has a high internet presence. Max uses the same format; mining her material from the volumes of e-mail she has received. Fortunately Max's area of expertise is in Film. And, though there is cross-over and grey areas, Television and Film are two different animals with the same genealogy.

So why would I mention it here? For the obvious reasons. Although many won't believe me, I developed this idea and structure on my own. So did Max. Elsewhere in this book I'll talk about how some ideas just happen to more than one person at a time, no matter how original you think it is. Well, this is a good case in point. You can accept this as truth or not, but I have a pretty strong bar for my own ethics. I give kudos to Max for acting on her idea immediately and getting it published. And if you like this format and want to see the Feature side of the business, I recommend that you give her book a look-see.

II. DISCLAIMERS, CAVEATS, AND COMMENTS

One of the things that I stress is that people who ask advice should take into account the experience and background of the people they get it from. So the first chapter of this book is who I am. And I suggest you search the internet for my credits. I would list them here, but I would have to update the book every year to keep it current. Besides, this book is likely to have the standard "Author's Bio" somewhere near the end, so you'll see some of them there. But, take my word for it, I've done a lot. I say this not to impress, but to put my words into perspective. At the same time I would never say that I know absolutely everything about writing or the industry; nobody really does. And I never have taken a class in either of those areas nor have I read books on them. Everything I know is based on my pure, practical experience.

I try to be honest and fair with this knowledge, but that comes with a price. The intent is that I firmly believe that a new Writer needs to arm herself with knowledge of the realities of the business. I can't and won't sugar coat it. I try to be encouraging and supportive, but the best thing I have to offer is honesty. Keep in mind that I am only the messenger. I'm not trying to be negative. And, in fact, much of you will read here is extremely positive. Some of it is, in fact, darn near optimistic and idealistic. A few of the anecdotes, for example, have stories that are sure to inspire and motivate you. Just keep it in perspective and don't forget the task at hand. One day you'll have your own anecdotes to with which to inspire. You have to get to that point first.

When reading this, keep in mind that though I have worked in many mediums, I am primarily a Television person. Television, Film, Animation, Digital Media, Stage and more, are distinct arenas, with different rules and interactions. I have written in all those areas, yes, but my primary area of expertise has been in the episodic world of Television. Remember that as you assign weight to my advice.

One of the problems with the Entertainment Industry (henceforth to be called simply the "Industry") is that there is very little quantifiable logic. It's a very subjective business and extremely unique to each individual. So what you should understand is that what I say here may be contradicted in the next book you read. It doesn't mean I am wrong or the author of the other book is wrong. It means that we have had different experiences and have drawn different conclusions. Research the authors of those books as I would expect you to research me. Again, you have to keep the knowledge within the context of the person it comes from.

Speaking of experience, in these many years of work, I've had more than a few. Experiences, that is. I find myself in the rather surprising position of having anecdotes about my life that others ask me to retell. So throughout this book, there will be several places where I will just stop everything and tell an anecdote from my own life.

These anecdotes may or may not have something to do with the chapter you are reading. And in these stories, when I have something nice to say about someone in the Industry, I will use their name. If it was a negative experience, chances are I won't. Why? Two reasons: One; just because I had a falling out or a bad experience with someone doesn't mean that they are a bad person or, even, that they were wrong. Your experience with them might be the complete opposite. And, two; I am still a part of this Industry, so I have no intentions of burning bridges anytime soon. In general, just consider the anecdotes to be mild distractions. There's a lot of stuff here and I don't want your eyes glazing over and rolling back in your head while you read it.

So when you reach an anecdote (clearly marked), you can either skip it and stick to the relevant information, or take a break and read it. Your choice. There will not be a test on the anecdotes.

Now, having just written the word "anecdote" more times in this chapter than I have ever used it in real life, let us proceed....

III. So, Who Are You?

Not you, *me*! The question is who am I! First of all, I'm not the kind of person who enjoys answering that question. Of all the things that are in this book, this is the most difficult to write. It requires a certain amount of objectivity that leaves modesty and self-deprecation in the closet. The best I can do is pile the modesty on the couch and try not to look at it. But before you can understand fully what I write here, you need to understand the perspective I have. This requires a little bit of info about me; where I came from, how I came to be a Writer, what my general attitudes are, and so on.

I don't expect anyone to follow my path, but if you do feel that some of my decisions are worth emulating, you should understand why I made them and how they came to play important parts in my life. That requires understanding who I am and, more importantly, why you are different. Your choices will (hopefully) be unique to you. Learn from me; don't learn to *be* me.

And I'll try to make this as painless as possible. For me, mostly.

Okay, now the hard part. I'm a fairly private person and I don't buy into the Hollywood-Self-Hype attitude. I was raised by loving parents who lived most of their adult lives as a military family. My father was in the U.S. Army and, as a result, we traveled quite a bit. Contrary to most beliefs among "civvies" (civilians), being in the Army doesn't mean you are a hardcore war-monger. Military Brats (as the children of military families are called) are more aware of the costs of conflict than civilians.

When I lived at Fort Knox, Kentucky, it was at the height of the Vietnam War. I know what it's like to be playing in your front lawn and seeing a moving van driving down the street. Everyone would stop and look, hoping that it was the result of a regular rotation and not because someone no longer had a reason to live on a military base. In other words, that a family had lost someone. What the military does give you, even as children, is a sense of discipline and responsibility. When I was a child, I didn't realize how important that would become to my later life.

One of the other things that a military family life brought to me was the fact that every three years, we would rotate out of one base to another. As a result, I have lived in Georgia, Florida, Kentucky, Germany and Washington (state) and we traveled extensively.

I've had a few people ask me if that was difficult as a child to move around that much. Perhaps for some, but I loved it. And it has given me a perspective of different people and cultures that I constantly refer to.

It also gave me an ability to quickly fit in to new situations. Let's face it; being the new kid in a school is difficult enough. Being the new kid in a school every three years requires some survival skills. You either become outgoing and extroverted or you retreat into solitude. I became the class clown. That was my survival skill. I made kids laugh and they accepted me. More than that, I enjoyed making people laugh. I enjoyed entertaining them. So where did this lead to?

Acting. I had the desire to perform in front of people. I was the first to volunteer for school pageants or skits. But I had a love/hate relationship with it. I didn't want people looking at me, I wanted them to look at the characters I played. Look at the mask, don't look behind it. I wanted people to enjoy the creativity, not the person. I'm sure there's a psychological term for that but, hey, I was just a kid, so who was thinking psychology? Anyway, when my father retired from the military, we move to St. Augustine, Florida. I was thirteen years old. I found out that the State Play of Florida (Cross & Sword) was holding auditions for their summer performance. I talked my mother into letting me audition.

The only thing I had memorized was the Gettysburg Address (from my Cub Scout days). So I got on stage and tried to emotionally interpret

Lincoln's famous reassertion of our country's freedom and dedication to liberty. As a thirteen year old. I'd like to think that somewhere, up above, Lincoln was smiling down on me saying "Ah! That's how I meant it to be said!" But let's face it; with my squeaky voice, it was less of an "Address" and more of a "P.O. Box." But it worked. I had my first paid acting job!

I performed in Cross & Sword for two years and began taking drama classes in high school. I loved it. And one of the things I loved most was the improvisation class. Improvisation is where you are given a situation and no script. You and one or more people are asked to perform the situation and "improvise" everything; character, actions, dialogue and whatever. For example, say that it's you and three people. The situation is: the four of you are on an elevator and it stalls. One of you hasn't showered in three days. Action. I loved this because it gave me a chance to create my character from scratch and play quickly off the characters the other people were creating. Relevant to writing? Yes, much more than you would think. Anyway, I soon became the head of the Drama Club at my high school and appeared in every production. Of course when I went to college, it was a given that my major would be …

… Medicine. I mean, hey, I loved acting, but I had to live in the real world! When my father retired from the military, he went into hospital administration (despite the fact that he was a front line soldier and not a doctor). He helped build a hospital in my hometown and I spent a lot of time there. I was always interested in science and medicine so it seemed like a logical direction for me to go. And it paid well. Acting would just be a hobby. Unfortunately, Medicine would also prove to be a hobby. Or, at best, an unfulfilled notion. You can't get into medical school with a "C" in chemistry. So Pre-Med quickly became Liberal Arts (which, I believe, in Latin means "I dunno"). This went on for a while. But all the time, I was still acting in productions and enjoying it.

So, now, one of those life-altering moments. Everyone's life is made up of moments. Points of intersection where a casual choice creates huge ripples in their life path. Fate dancing to random music; God rolling the dice; Destiny opening an unseen door. Or, in this case; Richard Dreyfuss.

In 1977, I was 19 years old and the movie "The Goodbye Girl" had just hit the theatres. Friends who had seen the movie were urging me to see it. They said, "The guy is playing you!" Now that's a careful distinction; he's playing ME. They didn't say I could have played that role, they said he was playing me. Intrigued, I went to see it. And, yes, I guess there was a lot of similarity to me (I even looked somewhat like him at that time). It certainly would have been a role I would have liked to play, but I logged it and forgot about it. Until … Richard Dreyfuss won an Oscar. For playing me! He won an Oscar!

Okay, epiphany coming. Shortly after he won the Oscar, I was walking from my dorm to the University Union center and I was thinking, "It's not like I'd have a chance. Only special people win the Oscar." At that moment, I stopped and got angry with myself. If Richard Dreyfuss had felt that way, he never would have accomplished anything! I looked around myself and realized that I had been confused over what I was going to do with my life when the thing I loved had been right there all along. I decided to change my major to Theatre!

I also had to tell my parents. Surprisingly, they were incredibly supportive. My father said "Well, you've always enjoyed it, so why not?" I was extremely blessed with these two people.

So, with that, I changed my major to Theatre and headed to the best Theatre School in the Southeast. Florida State University. This is not an idle brag on my alma mater, the school was, and has been, highly ranked as an Arts University. And, as an extension of that choice, I knew that I couldn't stay in Florida to pursue my career, so I had to move to New York or Los Angeles. Feeling that I wouldn't be comfortable in such a large compact city and would prefer something more spread out, I decided against New York and chose Los Angeles. The stage, so to speak, was set.

Okay, so how does all this lead up to a career as a Writer? The actual jump from Actor to Writer will be discussed later on, but again, to understand what I am saying, it's best you understand me and where I came from.

O   O   O

Anecdote Time: As a follow up to my Richard Dreyfuss revelation. The closest I had ever come to meeting the man was when I saw him in a restaurant once in the 1990's. I wanted to say something to him, but this was his private life. It wouldn't have been appropriate.

But in 2008, it was the time. It was the place. And I decided to talk to him. The place was the San Diego Comic Convention. It's the largest of the genre conventions and, though I've never appeared on a panel there, I usually go to hang out with friends and network. Not to mention the target rich environment as far as cosplay photography is concerned.

Richard Dreyfuss would be there, signing on a couple of those days, at a table in the merchandising area. My plan was simple. I was there with my girlfriend at the time and told her we would cruise by the table to see how he treated his fans. Some celebrities do signings reluctantly and, honestly, if he was a dick about it, I wouldn't bother. I was happy to see that he was engaging and charming, taking time to talk to people and listening to what they said to him. That was encouraging, so I decided to get in line the next day.

I showed up and stood in line, with my *Goodbye Girl* DVD to be signed (of course). My girlfriend brought a "Tin Man" DVD. When I finally got to him, we chatted a bit and I told him my story, of the role he played at a pivotal point in my life, of the decision that I made. I also told him where that decision had taken me. He listened and complimented me on the work I had done on *Xena*, saying that it had broken a lot of ground for others with its subtle but firm statement of equality (this particularly pleased me).

But what was really significant was when I told him my thought back then, that I'd never have a chance because "only special people win the Oscar." He smiled at me and said "It never occurred to me that I couldn't."

Although an Oscar has yet to grace my mantel, it doesn't matter. His response was exactly right. For myself and for everyone.

IV. WHAT KIND OF TOOLS DO I NEED?

Obviously, we aren't talking about carpentry, so I don't have a list of "tools" in the sense of hammers, saws, nails, etc. But the idea does apply to writing, if in a more esoteric manner.

Mechanically? You need something to write with and on. Pen and paper. A typewriter. A computer. Something. "Writing" is a verb. To make it a career, you can't just think it; you have to do it. Other than that … well, the rest is inside you. And it's more than just a great imagination. And since we are on that subject, let's start with …

Imagination—Before you get to the point of being a Writer, you have to be a storyteller. You have to be able to create stories. This comes from your imagination. You have to have a great fantasy life. You have to be able to look at things from a sideways point of view. You have to question everything and create answers for those questions. Imagination is something that we all have to varying degrees.

The key in being a storyteller is not only to imagine new and interesting things, it's a matter of being able to make those things interesting to other people. Hopefully, this started when you were a child. And, hopefully, you didn't lose it as an adult. Or, worse, that you, and others around you, didn't crush it. Being able to tell a story means you are willing to risk criticism. You are willing to risk looking like a fool. You'll take chances. Why? Because you want to tell a story.

Discipline—So much of this business is self-starting. There is no way to coast through it. If you haven't learned time management skills, start learning them now.

Procrastination is not just a problem in Hollywood; it's an art form. I can't tell you how many people have told me that they have a great screenplay idea and will get around to writing it some day. I can't say how many times people have told me that they intend to take a class on writing. Or they intend to follow up on an opportunity they had. Intentions don't mean anything here. It's the application that counts. And, yes, more times than not, your attempts will not result in accomplishment, but that's the business. You have to keep plugging away and you have to have the discipline to get off your butt and do it. Not because you are going to be rewarded immediately, but because it has to be done.

Along with this comes responsibility. You cannot blame anyone else for errors you make. No one cares.

You can't blame your lack of success on anything. That's the easy way out and leads to nothing. Yes, there are barriers to you. In fact, there are many more barriers in your way than you would find in other businesses. Some of them can be changed easily (i.e. learn to type), some of them can be changed with difficulty (i.e. move to Los Angeles if necessary) and some can't be changed (i.e. age and/or gender). I'll speak more on those examples later, but whatever difficulties face you, just acknowledge them and move on. Don't use them as a reason why you just can't make it. If that's your attitude, then don't even bother trying.

Outgoing attitude—This is important as, in the Industry (also known as "The Biz"), you will meet a lot of people. You have to learn how to quickly fit in and put them at ease. You have to become a part of their world easily. This is a combination of being friendly, attentive, humorous, assertive, and open. You want to give an impression of confidence and individuality while, at the same time, coming off as a member of the group. It comes down to this: You are a unique individual and you have value. Know this, understand this, and be comfortable with it. If you end up meeting Steven Spielberg at a party, you have to make it seem as if you have just as much legitimacy and confidence in who you are as he does while, at the same time, acknowledging his amazing success and talent. And, the hard part, it can't be an act. The Biz can sniff out fakers.

Be Adaptable and Open—Not just in your career, but in your life. In your career, this means that you have to be ready for anything and flow with the punches. Don't start fighting the good fight yet, you aren't even in the ring. Keep yourself open to opportunities that might appear, sometimes opportunities that are cleverly disguised. You are asked to help someone build a set for a local play. What does that have to do with writing? You don't know yet. But it does put you in contact with people who are also trying to get into the business.

Okay, sounds obscure, but I can point to incidents in my life where that kind of thing happened and led to things. Not always a job, but certainly to knowledge which is more valuable than a job at this point.

But, more importantly, I want to talk about staying open in your life and your goals. You may someday come to a "Moment of Decision." That means that at any moment, you may suddenly realize that you love something more than the thing that you always assumed you loved. How is this relevant to you? I mean, you already know you want to be a Writer, correct? That's true … for now. But you have no idea what kind of work you are getting yourself involved in. Even with that, you have to be open to find the thing that you love. You may start out wanting to be a Writer then, somehow, discover that you love being an accountant. If that's the case, don't be so fixated on the Writing thing that you completely ignore the thing that makes you happy.

"Happy" is what it's all about. I don't care what you say your goal is, whether to write for your favorite show, create a TV series, or write a blockbuster film, you are wrong. Your goal is a simple word: Happy. What you think of as your goal right now is your current belief as to what will accomplish that state of bliss. And that could, possibly, change. Have a direction and determination, but never lose sight of the "Happy" part.

There are way too many miserable people in this business, believe me. Many creative people fall prey to this because they get hung up on the whole "celebrity" aspect of the business. They may find that they actually hate it, but they stay the course because it was what they loved. Or what they continue to think they love. Being a Writer is not what you should be seeking. Being happy is the goal. If it means writing, so be it. But it could be something else. Don't close yourself off to the possibilities.

Understand Theatre—This should be a no-brainer, but it isn't always obvious. I think that Theatre is the best training ground for anyone who goes into Entertainment. Especially for Writers. The understanding of a play and why it works has incalculable value for a Writer. The understanding of Acting and Directing is just as important and in Theatre, the three areas of creativity are forced to work together (not always so in TV and Film, especially for the Writer).

And (big, big thing here) taking classes in Improvisation was the best thing that ever happened to me from a Writer standpoint. In Improv, you have to create a character, create a back-story, create involvement, create interaction with the other characters and create dialogue with little chance to prepare. Television, especially, requires quick reactions and quick thinking. When you do finally get into working on a series, you have to be able to do rewrites with very little time to prepare. And the writing of natural dialogue seems to be the hardest hurdle for new Writers to overcome. Mastering (or just being proficient in) Improvisation will give you the leg up over the competition. I suggest you look around for a class now. Take my word on this one.

At the same time, read plays. Read the classics. Understand play structure and storytelling from Shakespeare to O'Neill and beyond. Sure, you want to write for the "Barney Gill, Fish Attorney" TV series, but you'll still need to know the core elements of storytelling. Theatre and stage is the best place to learn it.

Self Confidence—This is not to be confused with arrogance. This means know who you are, know your limits and don't be afraid to walk away from things that bother you. The most powerful word you have at your disposal is the word "no." Why? Because everyone is willing to say "yes" in this business, but you really define yourself when you say "no." You set your boundaries and you let people know where you stand. Now, don't do it as a bluff or just to make a statement, but know what your core is and stand by it.

Don't delude yourself imagining how you'd like people to think of you, just be who you are and be confident in that. Self Confidence shines much more brightly than being a "yes" man. And it also inspires trust in you and your opinions. More than anything else, it will help protect you from the constant rejection you will be getting. Your ego has to be able to take that kind of abuse and the best way to defend against it is to know yourself.

With that, let's move on to …

V. THE BASICS

Before even considering a career in Screen-writing you have to think about the work involved in getting there. Just being able to type 120 pages does not make you a Writer, much less a Working Writer. To get to that point (and I am going to assume that is the reader's intent), you have to learn the craft and the business.

How do I learn to write?

The funny thing is that very few people ask this question. I saw a T-Shirt with the phrase "Writers Write." Nice thought, but even that can confuse creative expression with functional communication. Writing, for most people, is communication. Writing, for our purposes, is the creative expression of thoughts and ideas put into a structured format with the intent of creating a story to entertain and, if possible, to educate (try to put all that on a T-Shirt). The misconception is that because the vast majority of us can do the former, we assume we are capable of the latter. It isn't true.

Another version of this phrase is an answer I heard once at a party, when an aspiring Writer asked an established Writer "What is a Writer?" The established Writer responded "If you write, you are a Writer." Wow ... heavy ... very deep ... and total B.S. Phrases like this are part of the "Writer's Idealism" about their "Art." If you write, then you have acquired the basic language communication skills that anyone receives in public school. Being a Writer is something different. It's like saying if you paint, you're a painter. Well, then say hello to the Da Vinci putting a coat of green on your garage door. Writers don't understand they do a huge disservice to themselves and their profession when they go around spouting Writer's Idealism as quantifiable fact.

At this point, you have might noticed that I sometimes cap the "W" in "Write" or "Writer" and sometimes I don't. That's my way of making a distinction between the craft this book is about and the common school ability to communicate that we are taught. In short, all Writers who Write are writers who write, but not all writers who write are Writers who Write.

Truth is, Writing is a skill and, many times, an art. It is a craft and a profession. As with anything that falls into those realms, it takes knowledge and study.

You can't just jump into it, just as you can't just start building a house. There are a lot of things that you need to learn first, including things that will annoy or task you. You will have to learn things that seem to have little to do with your Storytelling and, therefore, you will think are unimportant details. Don't get yourself into that mindset. Writing for yourself is personal pleasure. Writing for a career is a BUSINESS. You need to treat it that way and handle yourself professionally.

The creative skill of Writing, the storytelling ability, is something that I don't think you can be taught. It can be developed; released; nurtured; but having it is a gift; a talent; an ability that is either there or it isn't. It's the soul of a Storyteller. Fortunately (or unfortunately) most of us don't know if we have it or not. In fact, most of us will never be sure. It's too subjective for us to quantify.

Assuming that you have it (and you do assume it, or you wouldn't be wasting time reading this), what you want to know is how that Storyteller's soul can be expressed in a script form that others can appreciate and enjoy. That involves two categories: The creative and the mechanical. To explain, the creative is designing a Porsche. The mechanical is making sure you have the necessary parts and instructions to assemble the car. The creative is a painting by Van Gogh. The mechanical is buying the canvas, assembling the paints and setting up the frame. But when it's time to fill that canvas with art ... get the idea?

To carry it further, the creative will stay in your mind, unseen and unappreciated by everyone, until you have a way to manifest it. In this case, we are talking about the Script. So for right now, we are going to talk about the functional purpose and format of a Script.

What is a script?

Many people have tried to describe the purpose of a Script in the filmmaking process. Some say that it is art; some say it is a blueprint. It's both (although I always have a problem with the "art" designation). In its final form, a Script, is a document that separates the various elements of production into easily identifiable sections for all departments of production. It lists the characters involved and, consequently, how many actors to hire. It lists the props necessary and the locations that need to be found. It gives the costuming department the guides to designing the wardrobe and indicates to the Director what kind of visuals can best interpret the Script. (Yes, all that falls on the shoulders of the Writer, long before anyone else gets involved.) Oh, yes … and the Script is also supposed to tell a story. To do all this requires a certain Script Format.

What is a script format?

Script Format is the way all these elements are arranged on the page. It is a structure that has no set rules and, yet, is very unforgiving to those who test the boundaries. It's a style that has evolved over several years and still maintained its basic look. Let's face it, though, if telling a story were the only purpose, it would look more like a novel. Which is why novels look like ... novels. The Script has a functional purpose that is beyond the mere creative expression.

I could go into minute detail about script format here, but there are so many research tools out there easily available to the average person. I'm not just talking about books that specifically teach script format, I'm talking about scripts! I'm amazed at how many people who want to be Writers have not taken the time to read scripts! They think that watching movies or TV will teach them what they need to know about scriptwriting. Big mistake. Watching movies or TV is supplemental to reading Scripts. What you see on the screen isn't Writing; it's the interpretation of a script by various people as a group effort into a final, visual, storytelling form. Before all that happens, you have to do your work; you have to write a script.

So go out and get some scripts. Important note: get produced scripts, not scripts written by other friends who want to break in. You want to learn from the professionals and, without slamming your creative friends, they have no more practical knowledge than you do.

There are various ways to get these scripts. One way is to search the Internet for production drafts. Production drafts are the actual scripts distributed during the production. If you can find original Writer's drafts, even better (though good luck on those … most of us hide them away from the public view).

Another way is to buy published scripts at bookstores. The problem with these scripts is that, most times, they aren't the production scripts. They are transcripts from the movie. The best way to tell this is if you watch the movie while reading the script. If the script matches the movie perfectly, then it is a transcript. Many things happen to the script along the way, many of them during the shooting and afterward during the editing. Scenes get lost, actors "improvise" lines, editing is done within scenes and, many times, entire scenes are created after the shooting to fill in gaps. But a transcript is perfect. If it's perfect, it isn't perfect for your use.

Okay, you have your script(s). Now you have to read them. Read them first just to enjoy them. Then go back and study them. Figure out why they work. Outline them. Scripts are made up of "threads." Aside from the major thread (the major storyline), each character has his or her own individual thread to follow through the script. There are plot threads, subplot threads, character threads, discovery threads, and so on. Isolate the different threads and see how they interrelate. Try to get into the mind of the Writer. Learn why things work. And, while reading the script, feel free to think of alternatives that the Writer might have considered while writing.

Another important thing to consider: You are reading the final form of the script. I can guarantee you, for every scene that you read, the Writer agonized over several scenes that she COULD have written and the geometric progression of alternates for subsequent scenes. The changing of one affects the whole script in a creative domino effect.

But back to format. Since I am talking about TV, I'm going to deal with the 60-minute episodic drama format, which is similar to screen format. Sit-com format is completely different and not in my realm of experience.

And if you have a production script, pull it out so you can follow along. If you don't, search the internet and bring up a few pages.

The first thing you might notice is that the script is divided up into segments; chapters, if you will. These "chapters" are called "Acts." There are also what is known as the Teaser and the Tag.

The Teaser—it's the opening of the episode. Most series have this, not all of them. It's the short bit before the title credits that gets your attention and sets up what you can expect to see in this episode. In a drama script, it might be no more than five pages long.

The Acts—These are the parts of the episode that are contained within commercial breaks. Each act starts after a commercial and ends before one. There can be anywhere between four and six act breaks for a sixty minute episode depending on the series. They are labeled Act One, Act Two and so on. The end of each act has to be compelling enough to bring the audience back after the commercial. Or, these days, keep the audience from channel surfing and finding something more interesting.

In the old days, a really riveting act ending would have the viewer rushing to the bathroom to take care of business and get back to their chair before the show began again. In the modern days of DVRs, strained audience bladders finally get some rest. But it doesn't change the fact that you have to bring the audience back after the commercial.

The Tag—The Tag is the end of the episode. Usually it is only three pages or so of wrap-up. The characters might discuss briefly what happened in the previous sixty minutes of the episode, wrap up any loose ends, or reflect on how the event has changed them. Again, not all series have Tags, but most do. Even without a commercial break, there is a rhythmic "tag" on each episode where these events occur.

That's the basic structure for the majority of TV shows out there ... now. The new paradigm of structure is a "no act" structure. You find this on networks that are not advertiser based. Such as HBO, Showtime and the like. You'll notice that in those series the structure is much more broad based and threads and events are more likely to be played out over the entire length of the series instead of in one episode. In other words, they play out more like a novel. This is a result of the serialization of TV. At one time, each episode of a series had to have an enclosed, self-contained plot and story that could be resolved by the end of the episode. This was so anyone who missed an episode, or wanted to start mid-season, didn't feel as if they had to play catch-up. Or, worse, just give up on the series completely because they felt lost.

But with the advent of DVRs, the Internet, Video On Demand and, especially, DVD box sets, that's no longer the rule. If you missed the first two episodes of a series, no worry. Look for it On Demand or streaming on the internet, or wait for the DVD box set.

For the Writer, it means we can spend more time investing in the story and characters over a longer period of time, much like a novel. Instead of Writing a series piecemeal, episode by episode, the entire season can be charted and scripted as an eight to ten hour movie. This new kind of storytelling has been difficult for many to adjust to, but it has created a surge in the quality of Television and, personally, I enjoy seeing it as a viewer. As a Writer, I absolutely love it.

Whichever structure, we are still talking about sixty minute episodes. So back to the script format. The page length of the script will be anywhere between forty-five pages and seventy pages. The general average rule is that it's sixty pages for a sixty minute episode. This is just a rule of thumb that should be forgotten as soon as you learn it. The true running length of a TV show (excluding commercials) is really less than fifty minutes, usually closer to forty. For the non-commercial series, the episodes can be a full sixty minutes (though they generally aren't). So it's just an approximation. Don't worry about it. *Xena: Warrior Princess* scripts, for example, were between forty and fifty pages. But other series would have seventy or more pages per script. Each show has its general length and that's what you should pay attention to.

Notice how each page of the script is divided up into different sections, segmented by different margins and placement on the page.

The dialogue is center of the page with the character's name in caps above it. The descriptive (also known as the "action") is in a paragraph form. Each "scene" is designated with a line in caps that tells you where the scene takes place; interior, exterior, location, and day or night (this is called the slug line). At the bottom of the page, you might notice the word CONTINUED (Mostly in old screenplays or TV scripts, in most current screenplays you won't see this).

You might also see numbers in the margins (scene numbers). At the top of the script, you might see a date and some sort of reference to color (green, blue, white, etc.) Those are revision dates and page colors to designate which changes were altered on which days. For your purposes, you don't need to worry about revision pages (since you are writing a script, not going into production) and don't number your scenes (that's for production, not for your draft).

You might notice a few other things, which I will mention because they are areas in dispute. First of all is the calling of camera angles. In a script, this is usually written as "ANGLE ON—*Xena*." It is the Writer's way of saying exactly what the visual angle in his mind was when he wrote it. Avoid this. That's the Director's job, let her figure it out. However, if there is something that is relevant to the story that you MUST be specific about, you could say "ANGLE— THE GUN UNDER THE DESK." In that example, you are reminding the audience that the gun is there because it is a part of the story, so you might need to specify the importance of this to the readers of the script. However, the best thing is to try and avoid it completely.

Next is the parenthetical. This is usually underneath the character's name just before dialogue.

```
            XENA
          (worried)
    Gabrielle, you should be here.
```

Some Actors don't like this as they feel it is telling them their job. Yes, it can be that. And most Writers use it as such, which makes the problem worse. There are Actors who go through their script scratching out any parenthetical because they find it insulting. Personally, I find this petty, but it's also arrogant when the Writer wastes time trying to manipulate the Actor into being a puppet. The real use of parenthetical is when the interpretation of the line might be in doubt as it pertains to the story. In other words, if there is a better than fifty-fifty chance that the line could be misread and, thus, affect the meaning of the dialogue, use a parenthetical. In other cases, leave it out.

Now, having said that, there this situation with calling camera angles and parentheticals puts the Writer between a rock and a hard place. That has to do with the people who read your script, not the Actors or Directors. Agents, Executives, the girlfriend of the Studio President and so on. The Writer's task is daunting. You have to write something that will never be appreciated as "Writing." It will go on to become a visual medium through the collaboration of many people. A Director will interpret it visually; Actors will give it breath; a talented crew will manifest it as reality for the camera. But before that happens, people, such as Studio Executives, have to read it first. More importantly, these Readers have to "see" it and "hear" it. That can only happen if the Writer writes in a visual/audio style that creates a movie in their heads.

The conflict here is that the easiest way to do that is to use camera angles and parentheticals in order to give the reader the correct visual and the correct readings. It's not that all Readers have no imagination, it's that you don't want them to spend their time working at visualizing the final product, you want them to sit back and experience it. So what to do? You write it in a visual/audio style, you run the risk of offending the Actors and Director. You don't do it and you run the risk of the Readers having a problem seeing the story.

Answer? Well … It's something that varies from situation to situation. If you have developed a script with the producers, chances are it has already been bought and will go to production. You can pull back on the angles and parentheticals. But if you have written a spec script, keep in mind that Readers have to read it first before it moves on to the Actors and Director. In that case, use what you need but use it sparingly. Only when absolutely necessary.

Margins. Such a simple thing, margins. As to the actual margins of the various parts of the script, they vary slightly from production to production. When writing a screenplay, you should follow a standard format. This means that you can just take your production script and copy the same margin settings, or you can get a book specifically on format and use those margins.

You can also purchase a scriptwriting program for your computer (highly recommended) that will have formats included with preset margins. Final Draft and Movie Magic are the two most popular, but there are many others. I have used all these programs and the one I prefer to use is Movie Magic. That's just a preference, you'll hear others rave about Final Draft for good reason. Other people are working with different programs or just using stylesheets. The truth is that whichever one you pick will be the best one for you, they are all very good.

If you are Writing a Spec Script for a television show, it's much easier to figure out the margins. You just get your hands on an actual script from that show and copy their format. Again, many scriptwriting programs will include formats for many popular TV shows.

What's a spec script?

A "Spec Script" is a script written on speculation. It is a script written to show your ability and talent in writing. In the feature world, it is a script that you wrote for free that you hope to sell. In TV, it's a script that you wrote for free that you will never sell, but hope to use to get an assignment. And, important thing, when I say "for free," I mean that you wrote it without pay or assignment; you wrote it on your own. Not because someone asked you to write a script for them for free (which you should never do in Television).

You've probably already picked up on the distinct difference between feature specs and TV specs. You can sell the feature spec; you can't sell the TV spec. The reason for this will be covered more in detail later.

What's an "A" plot? or a "B" plot?

They refer to threads in an episode. The "A" plot is the task, the mission, the experience the lead characters would be going through. The "B" plot is more character based. It can be dramatic or comedic. Ideally, it reflects the attitudes of the characters on something, usually the situation at hand. For example, the "A" plot might be detectives racing against time to stop a serial killer before he strikes again. The "B" plot would be how one of the detectives is dealing with a divorce at the same time. Or, if you want to tie it into the "A" plot, that one of the detectives lost his mother to a killer. You can have many subplots; C, D, E plots. But don't crowd them up so much that your script slows down and loses focus.

However, in the new paradigm of storytelling, the novelesque version I mentioned before, the character threads will be much heavier and extend much farther past the resolution of a particular plot point. In these series, the character thread is much more important.

What is a "Showrunner"?

This is the person at the top of the production chain on a TV series. The Executive Producer. It's this person's job to coordinate all the activities (or hire the right people to do that) and put together the series. This includes hiring the Writers, Directors, Actors and so on. This person also deals directly with the studios and networks.

What's the difference between staff writers and freelance writers?

In Television, there are two kinds of Writers: Staff Writers or Freelance Writers. Staff Writers are Writers who are contracted to a specific series and work for weeks or months with that show. They get a regular salary and can only write for that one series. A Freelancer (Freelance Writer) is a contract employee, working only on assignment. Those assignments may also be referred to as "Freelance assignments."

Obviously, most Writers would rather be on Staff than Freelancing. Aside from a steady salary, you are guaranteed to be writing scripts. The drawback to working on staff is that you cannot work on any other series except the one you are staffed on. A Freelancer can work on as many series as she can get work on. There just isn't any guarantee she will get all that work. Potentially, a Freelancer could write more scripts in a year than a Staff Writer. Each series has a limited number of episodes per season. Most staffs have four or five Writers and they have first shot at scripts before the Freelancer does. That doesn't leave many for Freelance. Another problem is that many shows don't hire Freelancers at all. So the assignments are sparse at best.

What about going to school to learn all this?

Finding a good school for Screenwriting will be your problem. There are many filmmaking schools around the country, but very few of them teach Screenwriting as an applied course. They may have courses, but the vast majority of those schools are focused more on hands-on production. Great for Directors; not so great for Writers.

However, I would still recommend a good film school for very important reasons. First of all, just because the school doesn't have an applied program doesn't mean it doesn't have an outstanding instructor. And, second, from what you've read so far, you should have picked up that in Writing a script the Writer has to be able understand the many different tasks that production will have to deal with. It would make sense that you would learn as much as possible about those other production jobs. I know many Writers who complain about things that happen to their scripts in production, but never take the time to learn why those things happen. Learn first so you can anticipate and, hopefully, participate in the solutions. Do this and you will be invaluable to the production.

Which schools have the best programs?

Hard for me to answer. I never went to school to learn any of this. True enough, I have never taken a course or read a book on Writing or production. I've never attended a film school. Don't take this as an indication of which path you should take, I was very, very lucky. I have also worked as a judge with the Academy of Television Arts and Sciences Student Emmy awards. This requires viewing finished short college films for award competition submitted by students at colleges and universities throughout the country. So I've had a chance to see what the different schools are putting out from their film programs. The consistent programs that I've seen over many years (as of this writing) are Florida State University, USC and UCLA. These are the names I have seen most often at the top, it is not, in any way, to diminish other schools. As a disclaimer, I got my degree in Theatre from Florida State University.

Do I need to go to college or just get started?

That's a personal choice. Yes, you could just get started. I, personally, think you should go to college for a number of reasons. One of them being that you could also learn a marketable trade to pay your bills while you try to break in (like a Business Degree). And, let's be honest, just in case you never do break in. Also, going to college gives you a chance to mature and learn that, quite possibly, this dream of being a Writer isn't what would make you happy. Again, don't be so fixed on the goal that you ignore other paths along the way that could be more rewarding.

And let me play "parent" for a moment. If you are asking this question, then it implies that you are young, probably still in High School. I'm going to say something now that you're going to hate. You are too young to be heading off to a career such as Writing. Now important note is that I didn't say that you are too young to <u>start</u> Writing. But a career is much more involved. And, with very very few exceptions, someone right out of High School doesn't have the social or business savvy to jump right in. I'm not being insulting here, but so much of life is learned by experience. Allow yourself that time to learn. College is a safe environment, a protected environment and allows you that learning without having to suffer the severe consequences of mistakes.

Here's a little test for you. Sit down with your parents and have them go through everything they had to do that month just to keep the household functioning. The budget, the bills, the food, the car maintenance, on and on and on. Have them show you the insurance premium for the house and cars and see if you understand everything about coverage and the definitions. Ask them how they deal with the phone company. On and on and on. If you can take on that burden without having to ask a lot of question to understand it, then maybe … maybe you have the life skills. When you are in college you are (hopefully) learning those things. You are (you're going to hate this) "maturing."

I know that you feel restrained and are eager to get out there and prove yourself, but, believe me, you have time. If you rush out too soon, you'll not only make mistakes, you'll be a prime target for people who want to take advantage of you. Right now, you're thinking "Hey, who does this guy think he is? I'm smart, I know my way around. No one's going to take advantage of me." That's a great attitude. And exactly what con men look for. I see this happen time and time again. So, advice from "Dad," take your time. Start your Writing now, start your learning now, but allow yourself time to grow into things. That's my opinion on the subject.

What's a "Newbie"?

You are. New to the business. AKA a "wannabee." I only mention those labels because you will run into them in this business and this book.

VI. Breaking In

There really is no set way to break into the business. There is no shortcut. It takes hard work and perseverance. It takes a thick skin. It takes an awareness of the realities that exist in the business of fantasy. You can't wait for opportunity to knock on your door. It's your job to find the doors to knock on. Most of them won't open. Many of the ones that do will slam in your face. You have to find the one that will stay open and, even better, invite you in.

I'm young but I've already made the choice to try and be a screenwriter. What should I do now?

Let's assume that you are starting from square one from outside Los Angeles. Some of this is going to touch on things I've already said, so consider those parts as being recaps because they are important.

So now that you've made the decision, what should you do and what should you expect to happen?

Obviously, learn how to write. Get scripts and read them. You've read me stating this before, but it's important enough to revisit. Again, not scripts that friends have written and not scripts that have yet to be sold. Get produced scripts. Learn the structure and format of scripts, but also learn that each script will be slightly different in structure and format. As you might have guessed already, the key is to study the scripts and analyze them as if they were text books. You can't make it a science, but treat it as one at the beginning. If you can, read the script before you see the movie. Then, when you do see the movie, go back, read the script again and make notes about what was different; not just in the translation, but in what you expected from the read and what you got from the visual. Always keep in mind that while you are writing something to be read, it's something that has to be "seen" visually in someone's mind.

If you haven't done it already, LEARN TO TYPE. Yeah, that sounds like a small and obvious thing to most people, but it's not a matter of just learning to type, you have to learn to make typing an unconscious part of your communication. A long time ago, I visited Santa Anita, the horse racing track. One of the jockeys there said something that relates to this. He noted that whenever you saw a jockey fall off a horse, that horse, now without a rider, seemed to run faster and, sometimes, beat the others to the finishing line. It's because jockeys are necessary to the race, but they don't do anything to make the horse faster, just the opposite. The way he put it "The jockey's job is to get out of the way of the horse." Same thing goes for typing on your keyboard. You want to get to the point that the keyboard gets out of the way of your creating. So the quicker you can get the idea from your brain to your script, the better off you will be. Typing has to become an unconscious part of the process.

At this point you might ask if it's absolutely necessary to actually "type" a script. Can't you just dictate it or write it out long hand to be transcribed later. The answer is, of course, yes. But if you do get an assignment for a TV episode, or manage to land on staff, you'll soon discover the pace of Television production doesn't allow for transcriptions.

You can expect to get some questions and disagreement about your choice of career. It may come from your parents or friends or lovers. They may want you to pursue other areas that are more stable. You know what? They are right. You should definitely pursue other possible careers, at least as a fall back. This is just common sense. Always keep in mind how this will affect your writing, though. Find something that will pay the bills but will still leave you time to write. And, as I've already stated, you might accidentally find something that you love more than writing as a career.

Now, the harder things about your choice of career are how the hard, cold business facts will affect you and your personal life. A Screenwriting Career is not just typing your creativity onto a page. It's as life altering as anything you will choose to do. And to do it successfully requires that you make choices, extremely hard choices that affect everything; repeat *everything*, that you now take for granted.

Plan now to move to Los Angeles. The most difficult thing to hear and for me to say. If you really want to break in, that's the place where it will most likely happen. And "most likely" doesn't mean "less likely" in other areas. It means "darn near impossible on your best days with all the Gods behind you in any other location." You are going to hear many many many many many many many many people tell you that you can write anywhere. That's true, you can do the act of writing anywhere. But actually breaking into the business and being taken seriously is another thing. More on this in a bit.

Also keep in mind that any life decisions you make (marriage, kids, etc.) are going to affect your career and vice versa. If you do find the person of your dreams and want to marry her, is she going to want to move to Los Angeles and deal with all the realities of that city? Is he willing to work, perhaps two jobs, while you try to work and spend your evening hours working on scripts? And is she (and you) ready for the reality that if you do sell a script … you are back to square one, unemployed and looking for another job? That's not the fear of Screenwriters, that's the accepted reality of it.

If you decide to have kids while trying to break in … you're crazy. Okay, maybe not crazy, but understand that your priorities in life will change (and should change) to accommodate the new (and more important) responsibility. This makes an uphill climb even more difficult.

If you have any vices to help you through your down periods or depressions (alcohol, drugs, etc.) keep in mind that you will become more dependent on them. Lose them now. This isn't moralizing, this is a fact. I know many people trying to break in who crawl into a bottle (pill or booze) because of the stress. They all tell me that when they break in, they will break those habits. It's not true. The pressure gets WORSE once you break in. Your escapes will scream even louder than before. You have to shake them before that happens.

Learn to balance a checkbook and manage your money. This isn't just common sense, it's crucial to your survival because of the fickleness of the industry. In other fields, people ask "What would you do if you became unemployed?" In Screenwriting, the phrase is "So, what do you do *when* you're unemployed?" Important difference. So learn how to spend and save your money so as to create a buffer for those long stretches. Never let your debt own you.

Do not attach yourself to material things. Two reasons: One is the obvious, you may have to sell everything you own to support yourself while trying to break in. And, two, living in Los Angeles, you'll most likely have an earthquake experience. People out here learn to make the distinction between what is luxury and what is necessary. Learn it now. It shouldn't be hard to remember that the priceless vase that has been in the family for generations isn't as important as your health and the friends you have. The question is whether that priceless vase is worth more than your career. If you have to sell it … will you?

Learn how to network. This is a necessary part of the business. You will go to screenings, parties, get-togethers, etc. and meet people. You have to learn how to network in the best possible way. This means casually associating yourself with people who may become a part of your world at a later time. It does NOT mean trying to show up at a premier so you can put a script into Spielberg's hands. Most of the people you network with will also be trying to break in. You don't want them to forget you when they do (and you shouldn't forget them in the reverse).

Also, learn that arrogance is no substitute for talent. There will come a time in your life when you think that you are just too hot for words. At that point, you will be taken down a few pegs. How you recover is important. You are not, and never will be, the top dog in the pound. Having confidence in your abilities and talent to back it up is more than enough to gain the respect you need.

Learn how to watch the world and ask questions. Don't EVER let anyone take that away from you. Always play "what if" in your mind. Don't take things for granted; spin stories about anything that tickles your fancy. That doesn't mean writing out a complete story, it means small things as well. When I'm out and about the public, I am constantly making little scenes out of things I see. I see two people with a doughnut and I imagine what they are talking about, what's the importance of the doughnut, and so on. I'll create an entire scenario around just two people talking with one of them holding a doughnut; their past, their history together, what they are discussing, everything. Then, I take it one step farther and I try to figure out how the doughnut would tell the story.

Yeah, that's what I'm like. It's more than just a source of personal amusement, it keeps my mind in a creative mold.

To that, remember that the creative part of your mind is a tool that improves with use and decays without it. Always stimulate your mind. Read. Not just scripts, but READ! Challenge yourself to learn something new every day.

When you can, seek out people with experience and ask advice. There is book knowledge, and then there is learned knowledge. Books are good and you should absolutely read about the business. But the learned knowledge gained from someone's experience has more significance in your life. At the same time, you have to weigh the advice you get and credibility of the people you get it from. This is not to negate the advice of people who haven't the experience, but you have to learn to put it into perspective. And even with people who DO have experience, they aren't you and you won't follow their path. You have to listen to many people, figure out what makes sense, and figure out what works for you.

Can I break into writing without moving to Los Angeles?

Before I get into this, I want to make an important distinction. I would be remiss if I didn't mention the difference between Film and TV in regards to breaking in. In film, the SCRIPT is the object for sale. In TV, YOU are the object for sale. That's it (more or less). You don't sell spec TV scripts, so what you are selling is your ability to write a script. And to do that, the Producers have to know if they can work with you. Not just your talent, but what you are like to work with on a day to day basis. This requires a personal interaction and, even more, an ability to take meetings. Keep that in mind, you are selling YOU, not a script. Why is that important to know? It's at the core of the answer to this question.

This is the most upsetting topic for most people. It's very discouraging and, let's face it, most people have too many responsibilities to just uproot and move to Los Angeles. I could lie to you and say that anything's possible. But I feel that knowledge is a better weapon than optimistic ignorance. So, please, this is the darkest chapter in this book and I ask you to just bite your lip and barrel through it to the end. There's still info that can help.

Breaking into the Television industry as a Writer is an extremely difficult task in the best of situations. And when we talk "extremely difficult," we're on the same level of "I want to play professional sports for a living" difficult. And that's just getting an assignment, much less having a full career.

Now make it 100 times more difficult.

You still aren't there yet.

The sad truth is that it is next to impossible, from a standing start, to break into the business of Television Writing without being in Los Angeles.

Most books won't tell you that; I just did. But knowledge is power, so let's read on to figure out why that's true.

I've had many agents and I've asked almost every one of them what their policy was on out-of-L.A. submissions. The response has been the same; unless it is off a recommendation with high credentials, it is dismissed out of hand. The receptionist and secretaries, when taking a phone call query from out-of-L.A. are instructed to tell the caller "we're not seeking new clients, but if you move to L.A. please contact us again." This isn't an invitation, it is a polite dismissal.

Even the winners of national screenwriting competitions will get the "when you move to L.A." comment.

The exceptions … yes, we can all come up with names of people who broke into the system from out of L.A. Most of the times though, under careful scrutiny, we'll find something that explains it. A published novel, for example. A relative who is an Agent or is the lawyer of an Agent, etc. A person in the right place at the right time knowing the right people. But for breaking in from a standing start from outside L.A.? Extremely rare.

Even then, people will struggle to find an exception. But, for some reason, they seem to forget that it is an "exception." And (here's where the disconnect is) it's rare in a business where breaking in under the *best* of conditions is rare.

Does it mean you absolutely cannot break in from out of L.A. from a flat start? No. Is there any reason you can't empty Lake Superior with a teaspoon? No. Theoretically they are both possible. Theoretically.

But wait, you say (go on, say it), MY spec script is special! MY script is so good they can't possibly ignore it! MY script will stand out from the rest! *Yawn*. Maybe. Maybe not. But here's something else to think about. In the studio/Agent/network system, there is only one person with the power to say "yes." The only power the people below that person have are to say "no" or "I don't know, so someone above me needs to read it" (which by the way, is their version of "yes"). That, in itself, wouldn't be so bad except for that executive/assistants' primary responsibility: to keep their job. Keeping their job means having to second guess their boss's subjective preferences and prevent themselves from looking like someone who doesn't know the difference between a good script and a bad one.

Now reread what I just wrote. Not because I think you're stupid, but because it takes a moment to digest.

What it means is that the lower people (everyone under the "Yes" person) are just as motivated by looking for scripts to move up the chain as they are looking for reasons NOT to move scripts up the chain. Rejecting scripts isn't a risk. Accepting them is. That's when your reputation is on the line. So when they have hundreds of scripts to wade through (and they do), finding one with an out of L.A. address is a no brainer. It's a safe reject.

Horrible, isn't it? Even now, most of you are thinking that it's horrible that I would become so jaded that I would think this is the way it's done. First of all, it happens most of the time. And, secondly, I've seen it in action.

Again, like everything else in this business, there is no standard. There are execs who do take chances. There are execs who find great scripts and have the enthusiasm to really push them to their bosses. I'd like to think that every person who takes that route does it for sincerely creative reasons. But for many of them, the business soon becomes less about creativity and more about politics. They have to hold onto their jobs. Many established Writers complain that studio execs are so young. They rarely ask the obvious question of "why?" Do they burn out early? With all the stress, it's very possible. Are they subject to ageism as well? Yes, they are. Or are the ones who continue in the business better at politics? For the most part, yes. None of the preceding has anything to do with finding good scripts. Sadly. But it also doesn't mean that the execs don't want to find good scripts because no one knows where the next superstar series creator is going to come from.

I have a lot of respect for what execs have to go through, believe me.

But back to you and your situation. Why Los Angeles? Networking is extremely important in the Film and TV business. Most of the breaks you get will come as a result of networking with people, whether at parties or casual events. Hollywood is a very interactive business. You can't get that kind of networking potential anywhere else.

Further, face-to-face time is of extreme importance. You have to be available for meetings. At a moment's notice. And, most importantly, you have to expect that those meetings are going to be postponed at the last moment, many times when you are pulling into the parking lot. THIS IS NOT HYPERBOLE. You are starting out; your meeting is expendable. Even when you are established, your meeting is expendable. To those who say they can fly in for meetings, let me put forward this scenario.

You have, somehow, managed to get a meeting with X for Tuesday at 11:30 a.m. You'll have to take Tuesday off and fly in that morning, leave that evening. As the meeting was set up just five days prior, you'll have to pay top dollar for your ticket (or hope you have Frequent Flier miles). So you fly in, get your rental, and drive to the meeting ....oh, wait. X has an emergency meeting he has to attend. We'll call you back.

Sometime around 2 p.m. you have to make a decision, cancel your flight back? You call the office to get a time. They don't know, they'll call you back. You tell the assistant that you have to fly back, she sounds apologetic but will let you know when she can. Around 4 p.m. you have to decide what to do. Your plane leaves at 7 p.m. You call again. Oh, sorry, but X went home early. We'll have to reschedule. Angry and frustrated, you want to scream at the assistant and write an angry letter. But you can't because you'll blow your chance. So you make your plane and fly back home. And when you get there, you have a message waiting telling you that your meeting has been rescheduled for Thursday.

And the funny thing? There's a fifty-fifty chance that Thursday will be a repeat of Tuesday.

You're now thinking that I'm playing "parent" here by using a worst case scenario in order to make the point. No, ask any professional in this business.

This isn't a worst case scenario, this is BUSINESS AS USUAL. I cannot stress that enough. I have this happen all the time, it's just accepted. I live here, so it's an annoyance at best. But how long could you continue to do this?

By the strangest of coincidences, just as I was polishing that last paragraph, I got an e-mail telling me that, yes, my meeting at the studio for next Monday has been postponed. No lie.

Unless you already have a contact in a hiring position or someone who has heavy input into the hiring of Writers, there is no way you are going to be taken seriously if you aren't in Los Angeles. Even if you have an incredible spec script, it's not going to happen.

TV is a more immediate business than features and the face to face is crucial. That means that they want to have you in the room so they can work with you.

Now let me go through a few of the arguments that might pop into your head.

"Maybe that used to be true, but this is the 21st century! We have the Internet, FAX machines, inexpensive phone calls, etc."

It's still true. In the "old days" we had phones. And we had FAX machines. And it didn't matter. An office meeting is more than just an exchange of information. It's people who bounce off each other. Ever seen one of those inflatable rooms that you can rent for parties? They have lots of beads or balls in them so that kids can jump up and down inside them?

Well, a creative meeting is just like that, except the things bouncing around in the room are your ideas; your notions; your creativity. Now imagine being on the outside looking into that bouncy room. All you can do is react after the fact. You can't participate. A meeting is a creative bouncy room. And you need to physically be in it to be a part of it.

"What about shows like the old Star Trek; The Next Generation? They hired people from out of state. They even bought spec scripts"

The Star Trek "open submission policy" is only remarkable because of one thing: It existed. It was an anomaly. And, if you really examine it, it was intended more toward the fans, so they could feel a part of the Star Trek experience. But even if it was more than that, we only talk about it because it was incredibly rare. It's not the norm.

"I know a guy who writes from New York"

And chances are he's already established in the business. He already has his contacts and can afford to work from another state. But he didn't get started that way.

"I can fly in for meetings"

This has various versions such as "I can fly in for meetings at a moment's notice" or "I can fly in for meetings if it's a serious meeting." Let's discount the latter first: none of the meetings are serious until you get paid, and all of them are serious even if you don't.

As to the "I can fly in at a moment's notice," that works in a perfect world. And, maybe, in any other business. But not in this one. I've already elaborated on how a meeting gets moved on a regular basis. How many days off can you take? How many frequent flyer miles have you got? How much wear and tear can your psyche take with this treatment?

"They are shooting a series near my hometown. I can submit to them, can't I?"

You can, but it won't mean anything. The Producers and staff are usually back in Los Angeles. The only remote possibility is some shows that are shot in New York. Even then, they are looking to Los Angeles first. Why? Because whether it's fair or not, they figure if you aren't in Los Angeles, you aren't serious about being a Writer.

Let me put it this way; with all the shows I have worked on staff (Writer/Story Editor/Producer), all of them since 1987 have been shot outside of Los Angeles (a sad commentary on runaway production). And in all that time, I can only think of TWO Writers we hired who didn't live in Los Angeles. One was a friend of the Executive Producer and lived in New York. The other was someone I had worked with before and lived in Miami (note that both of them had previous contacts). But that's it. Only two. And we're talking many shows and several hundreds of episodes.

"It shouldn't matter if I can get an Agent or manager who lives in Los Angeles"

The Producers don't have to work with the Agent or manager, they have to work with you. See above comments about that. And, as I've mentioned, agents and managers usually share the opinion that if you aren't in Los Angeles, you aren't serious. Agents I have talked to on this subject have told me that they have a "not accepting clients" letter they send out (if they bother to send anything at all) and one of the things that triggers that letter is an out of state postmark. In fact, I'll go one step further and say that if an Agent or manager does want to take you on, I'd be very suspicious of a con job (more on that later).

Many will think that Hollywood is missing out on some great talent by only shopping L.A., that it's extremely unfair. And those people are wrong on both accounts. TV is a business. And the business has to run smoothly to work. It's not unfair because it follows strict rules that have evolved over many years. They may have little logic, but they are practical. And talent means nothing if it doesn't fit smoothly into the machine. Hollywood doesn't go searching the world for talent, it can't afford to. And it doesn't have to. It can just stand there, like the monolith in *2001*, and wait for our primal ancestors to dance around it. It doesn't have to move. The australopithecines will come. Why? Because that's where the monolith IS.

With all that, why is there still this argument about being in L.A. versus breaking in from another state? Because for most of us, the sad truth is that we have no choice. When I moved out, I had nothing to hold me back. I had no attachments to my home town, no wife, no kids, nothing but myself to support. In short, I had no responsibilities. But what if you have a spouse or kids or a job that pays you well enough to have things that you enjoy? What happens when, despite all that, you have this burning desire to break into a business that requires you to go back to square one just to get an even break?

You feel trapped and frustrated and grasp at any remote possibility of a chance in order to believe that you can still "have it all." I wish it was true, but it isn't. You have to make choices, difficult ones. And the choices we make don't always go easily with ones we'd like to make.

So where does that leave you? Just where you are. You'll continue to write your specs, continue to seek out "short cuts," continue to make submissions and continue to argue that it can be done and you're the one to do it. Why? Because you have no other options; you have this urge to write. The only real chance you have (and, again, it is slim to none) is to write your spec screenplays and hope that SOMEHOW you can get them noticed enough to sell one. See if your area has independent films being made or independent filmmakers. Approach them about producing one of your scripts. You may not get rich doing this, but it will give you some satisfaction and, maybe, some credibility to get you noticed. If you are rich, finance your own film (not so bizarre, I had a friend who did that).

I would ask all of you to avoid ignoring all the things you DO have. If you DO have a family or a well paying job and a nice home, please don't easily dismiss them out of hand because of this "dream" that you have. Write your scripts, make your submissions, but don't forget to kiss your spouse, hug your kids and enjoy your weekends off. You have more than you realize and you'd be the envy of many in this business because of it. Don't take it for granted.

O O O

So. Now that I have completely depressed you and you're coiling the rope (either for me or yourself), let me add this. I WANT YOU TO PROVE ME WRONG! Just because I told you the reality doesn't mean you should give up and stop trying. Hell, I told you all that so you would be better armed or, at least, better informed. You are now ready to make REAL decisions, not ones based on fantasy and hope.

So cue the happy-dance music and let's do some more exploring.

The Internet is not the answer to this. But it is a really good step in the right direction if you know how to use it. It has vastly improved our ability to interact with each other and it's getting better every day. When it was just e-mails, yeah, you were pretty much screwed. But now we have instant text, face-to-face conferencing, and the like. We also have social networking where we can interact and contact others of a like mind. We have groups on various websites where Writers congregate. And, many times, the aspiring Writers interact directly with established Writers and Producers.

Remember I mentioned one of the examples of an exception? Someone I hired who lived in Miami? Well, I met her through the internet. Now, granted, there were some exceptional things that had to fall into place for her to go from an internet friend to a Writer on my show, but it did happen. She was a fan of a series and I interacted with the fans online. She was also known for the fan fiction she wrote and she became very popular. Her writing was very good. So when the Executive Producer of the series told me that he wanted to try something different and hire a fan to write an episode, then asked me to recommend someone, she got the call.

What are the odds of that? Well ... pretty slim for the average person. But it still happened.

Also, keep in mind what I said at the beginning of this chapter. The difference between screenplays and teleplays. In Television, they are buying YOU. In features, they buy the script. That means that they don't really care where you live, they are looking at your final product and will buy that. And if you can get a feature script sold, well, you now have access to the industry. You also have credibility. And if your screenplay becomes a major film, you'll have an Agent and offers.

But slow down, Bucky, selling a feature isn't easy either. But you don't have more of a chance relative to getting a Television assignment. So why not?

So my advice for you, if you can't make the move, is to still write your scripts, but also get involved as much as possible with the industry and industry people through the internet. Write in other mediums and get those out there, whether it's novels or comics or whatever. And screenplays. Don't forget that.

And don't let someone like me tell you you can't do it.

Why shouldn't I send a spec script to the series that I wrote it for?

I said I would get back to this. Earlier, I explained what a spec script is. I also said that one of the differences between a Film spec and a TV spec is that you can sell the Film spec, but not the TV spec. You might just be thinking that writing a TV spec seems like a waste of time if you can't sell it. In TV, spec scripts are intended as a sample of your work only. A tool used to sell yourself. In fact, specs should NEVER be sent to the series that you wrote it for with the blind idea that they might just buy it.

TV Series don't buy scripts, we buy Writers. We want to bring in a Writer, hear a pitch, buy a story and develop it with the Writer. It has nothing to do with ego, it has to do with the speed of Television and the careful crafting of stories and characters. Film companies buy scripts. They have less use for the Writer once they own the script (sad but true). The script is finished, here's your check, stop in at the gift shop on the way out. Done. Not so in Television.

Look at it this way: If I am running a series, I live, eat and breathe that series twenty-four hours a day. Everything I come into contact with is interpreted through that series. I hum the theme song on the way home. The same with other Producers and staff. They are privy to every meeting that discusses every nuance of the series. And, more than anything else, they are in production mode. So every bit of their existence has some attachment to that series and the production of it.

When your script comes across their desk, if it is for their series, two things happen. They automatically start assigning all their rules and nuances of the series to your script. These are things you couldn't possibly know and certainly couldn't know to the depth that they do. The bar for judging your script, on that alone, has just shot up to dizzying heights. Add to that the fact that that script will also subconsciously be judged not as a spec script, but as a production script. Why? Because that is where the mind of the Producer is at that moment. So every small detail becomes a red mark. There is no subjectivity in which to just simply judge the writing and the Writer's ability.

There is NO WAY you, an outsider, is going to be able to hit that mark no matter how good you think it is. It doesn't sound fair, but it is human nature.

What you want to do is send a script from a show that is similar to the one you want to get a meeting on. And by similar, I mean as similar in tone and characterizations as you can get. When I get a script from another series, I can't read it from a production viewpoint, I am forced to evaluate the *writing*. And that's what you want me to do.

See, what you are showing me is that you are a competent Writer with your spec script. I can then teach you the intricate and subtle details of our particular show. If you send me a spec script for my series, you are telling me that you already know those subtle details (and you won't). And even if you say that you are willing to change them, you have already shown your disposition toward the series. We generally find it easier to teach than unteach. Again, fair? Well … in this business, yes. Fair to the series and the precious time we have to service the writing.

O   O   O

Anecdote Time: When I started out, I had a writing partner, Burt Pearl. You're going to read more about this story later, but we called Cannell productions and asked for the Writer's Guidelines for their new show *Riptide*. The assistant we talked to told us to send two samples of our work, but NOT a *Riptide*. Now, we had a *Riptide* spec, but we trusted her judgment and sent two other series instead. We got a meeting. We pitched. We got a story assignment. We got the script option. We got on staff. Once we were comfortably on staff, I mentioned to the Producer that we had a spec *Riptide* script. Now we had NAILED this script. It was perfect for the show. He asked to see it. He read it and told us "If you had sent us this spec, we never would have met with you."

But we were sure we had NAILED it! No, we hadn't. So no matter how much you think you have the perfect script for a particular series, no matter how tempted you are to send it … DON'T. Those spec scripts are your calling card, a demonstration of your talent. They are tools of your trade to get you work. And your work (in TV) is a service you provide, not an item that you sell.

I have a spec script for a cancelled series. Is it still any good?

The out-of-date spec script is something that is a pain. The other annoying thing is when you've written a script revolving around a certain character or situation and the series kills off that character or changes the situation. That's happening a lot more with the new paradigm of serialized series.

What do you do? Go back and rewrite the entire spec script? Well, if you can easily do it, then do it. But you can't spend your career chasing the **tail of the dog.**

First of all, you aren't writing your spec to be produced for the series. And you are NOT going to send your script to the company you wrote it for, remember? But what you are expected to do is …

Nothing. You aren't expected to do anything. When a Producer gets a script, he isn't reading it as an audience member trying to follow the continuity of the series. He's not sitting there saying "This can't be used on that series, this character just died!" In fact, chances are, he's not even watching that series. And he's not going to go around asking people if your script doesn't fit the series anymore.

No, what he's looking for is your writing. Can you write an episodic script? That's the bottom line.

Now there is a general rule that I have found to be true. If there is a major change in the series arc, your spec script has a one to two year lifespan as a result. It has nothing to do with your writing ability or your keeping up with the series. It has to do with dating your spec. Producers don't like to see scripts that are two years old, they'll ask for something more recent. So you must always keep writing specs (or, at the least, keep updating your specs).

Another suggestion, and one that I personally recommend, is that people write one hour pilot specs. It's original and won't go out of date (with the exception of advancements in technology and such). A few of the panels I have been on with other Showrunners have said the same thing. In fact, funny thing, I was on a panel where this question came up and we all responded that we would read spec pilots. Someone in the audience had gone to the panel just before ours, a panel of studio execs. And, apparently, the studio execs had said NOT to write spec pilots. One of our people promptly responded "They don't generally hire you ... we do."

Writing a spec pilot, however, isn't as easy as writing a spec episode of an existing show or, even, as easy as writing a feature.

How do I write a pilot? What are the differences?

Ah, this is an area that is hard to discuss. It's something that takes, probably, 75% experience, 20% luck and 3% instruction (the other 2% is coffee). And even though I might recommend you write a spec pilot, I also caution you to be very careful when you write one. They are not easy to do and very easily done wrong. It's not like writing a spec episode of an existing series. In the existing series, you already have your characters in place and your settings established. The guest stars and alternate locations are cursory at best because you are concentrating on the established things in the series to tell the story. In other words, 70% of your work is already done (I use instructional percentages a lot, on average 60% of the time). But in a pilot, you have to establish all those things; the characters, the locations, the franchise of the series, and continuing threads. Okay, so let's break this down.

Characters—Easy enough, your main characters. You need to introduce them in the same manner that you might introduce a new character in a screenplay. You know your audience has never seen them before and knows nothing about them. You have to establish who they are in immediate and in extended ways. For example, an immediate way would be that the character wears an eye patch. The extended way would be how he came to wear that eye patch and how it affects the character's day to day actions. You also have to establish the character's interactions with her surroundings and other characters. But to go back to the differences between episode and pilot, you are dealing with an unknown as far as the audience is concerned. Not only do you need to give the audience a sense of who the person is, you need to establish a sense of "we want to follow this character around." Especially the lead character. If the character were not special in this regard, he or she would not have a series.

The Locations—Again, easy enough. It's the regular hangout(s). If it's a cop show, it might be the police department. If it's a law show, it might be the legal office. But in all shows, when you are dealing with characters, you will also have to deal with their home environments. Keep in mind that describing that environment can go a long way in describing your character without having to have a lot of expository dialogue from characters. There's an old adage that you can tell a lot about people by looking at the book titles on their shelves. It's true. Use that device. Don't go into major detail about it in your description, but a few well crafted phrases can say much with little. For example, the Lawyer. His office might be described thusly: "Walking into Jeremiah's office is much like walking into the Huntington Library. Darkly leather bound books surround the corners of the room, leaving little room for the dark mahogany desk with the single lamp." Okay, that has already established an image in your mind of Jeremiah's office, but it also tells you a bit about him. He is a pure lawyer with a reverence for the written law. He is a traditionalist in his approach to his profession. Now, however, we go to his home: "Jeremiah's home is a contradiction to Jeremiah himself. A collection of metal and glass, DVDs and CDs sit mostly on the shelves, many on the floor. He kicks through the discarded clothes on the floor as he heads to his bedroom." Okay, now you have learned that Jeremiah has a dichotomy in his life. His professional legal appearance is a pretense, a concession to his career. The real world, as reflected by his home, is very much different. With those two descriptions, I have given you a fairly clear image of this man by using his chosen environments. Use this method when you create the world of your characters.

The Franchise of the Series—This is a little harder to describe because I have to assume you have no idea what I am talking about. The franchise is the "thing" that makes this series what it is. And it could very well sound shallow because, in most cases, it has little to do with character and mostly to do with location or situation. For example, the series *Cheers*. The franchise was the colorful people and their interactions in a Boston pub. *M*A*S*H* was the day to day existence of an Army mobile surgical unit in Korea during the war. *Six Feet Under* is the story of a family run Mortuary. Those are "franchises."

Continuing Threads—In a screenplay, you set up threads at the beginning of the screenplay: character quirks, running gags, subplots, things that the screenplay will bring in and out as needed then, at the end of the movie, resolve for the satisfaction of the audience. Not so in pilots. Remember, you are setting up a series. Which means the end of your pilot is really the beginning of the series. In other words, the end of your pilot is only page twenty of the screenplay. So many times, threads need to be set up that don't get resolved in the pilot. They get played out over the life of the series. They may occasionally become episodes in themselves, but they aren't meant to be wrapped up neatly. There are character issues left hanging at the end of the episode. Those things will be touched upon later in the series. They aren't intended to come to a definite conclusion. These things can make the characters more human and engage the audience on a personal level.

The key in all of this is to not try to do it all at once. Again, the pilot script is the beginning. It's the set up. It has to have its own plot to be resolved, but that has to be within the framework of setting up the characters, locations, franchise and threads.

Of course, writing a pilot script isn't the final step. You have to sell the darn thing. We'll get to that later.

How do I make my script stand out?

Okay, I'm going to ramble out some thoughts here about the whole Spec script thing and access to the people who can get you into a meeting.

So, you're wondering, how do I make my spec stand out? Well, that is simple. Write a great script. Hopefully, that's your goal anyway. How you make that script great takes a lot of study and experience. You need to get your work reviewed and critiqued. You need to put your ego on hold as you objectively look at your baby and the responses and put it all together into a creative, interesting, commercial viable product.

Not the answer you expected? Well, it's because all scripts that go out are expected to be great. You shouldn't send one out if you don't think it is. So the question isn't really how do you make it stand out, it's how do I get them to see it? The problem is getting your script read in the first place.

The best answer? Have a great Agent, have a friend who's a Producer, yada yada yada yada. But assuming you don't have that, here are some things to keep in mind when you work on your specs.

DO NOT write a spec script for the show you are submitting it for. I've covered this already. So moving on—

Send a script that is appropriate to the show you are submitting to. For example, a *Game of Thrones* script wouldn't be a good choice for *CSI:* You might send a *Law & Order* script instead. It's in the same genre and more in line with *CSI:* sensibilities.

You'll want to submit to many different series, so write many spec scripts of different styles to cover a wide range. That may sound like a lot of work, but it's absolutely necessary. You need at least five spec scripts of different styles before you even start out.

Most Producers only read the first ten to fifteen pages. Why? Because we don't have time to read the whole script! We have a stack to get through. In twelve pages, I can tell whether someone has what it takes or what I need. Some of us read the first twelve pages (I do) and some just open the script in the middle and start reading. So you have to make sure that your entire script is riveting and engaging. On very rare occasions have I been compelled to read the entire script. It's happened and, in some cases, I have been impressed. In others, I have been disappointed to realize that the beginning of the script was all they had.

Most TV Producers concentrate on Dialogue rather than story. And by dialogue, I don't just mean the natural pattern of speech. I mean how ideas and concepts are delivered without sounding "written" or expository. How the characters interact with each other in a natural way. Those kinds of things. Yes, the story needs to be interesting, but I intend to work with you on your story. I will be able to help you form your outline so that the story will be solid. However, when you go off to write those scenes, I have to feel comfortable that you can deliver those characters as naturally as possible. Time and time again, you will hear people say that they were impressed by someone's dialogue in their writing (MAJOR REMINDER: This is where your class in Improvisation will make you shine).

This is not to say you can slack off on your story. Most studio executives pay more attention to story. Your solution is to do both things exceptionally well.

Not all Producers are as obvious as their series. For example, if you look up my resumé on IMDb (the Internet Movie Database), you'll see that I have a lot of "action" series on it. But if you read my scripts, you'll note that I spend more time working on my characters. I like character stories. I like to write them, I like to read them, I like to see them. I have always referred to my episodes as "Character stories *with* action." For me, I can write action in my sleep. I actually do choreograph my action scenes in my scripts and it's not a big deal. Character, though, that's much more difficult. And I look for people who can handle that.

Now, how are you supposed to know that? Here's where the research comes in. One relatively easy way is to go to seminars and panels with Showrunners. ASK them what they like to read. More importantly, take notes on EACH INDIVIDUAL. Most people just take general notes, looking for some sort of consensus among us all. It isn't like that. We all have particular tastes and you should know what they are.

That way, when you are ready to send me a spec, you can look in your notes and see "Steven L. Sears ... likes character based scripts with twenty dollar bills paperclipped to the cover." If you can't make it to seminars, do internet searches for interviews with people and make a profile for your records. It will really come in handy.

How do you get to talk to the people you need to talk to? Well, again, I would recommend seminars and the like. Many of these panels have dessert and coffee afterward for mingling with the guests. Take advantage of it.

Also, here's a "secret" that USED to work (but it might not work as well now). Call the office of the Story Editor, but try calling during the following hours: 7 a.m. to 9 a.m., 11:30 a.m. to 1:30 p.m., 6 p.m. to 7 p.m. Why? because these are the times that the office staff will most likely be out of the office. And if the show is in production, these are also times that the writing staff might actually be IN the office and picking up their own phones. These days, it's a long shot, but worth a try. I got to talk to a lot of people this way when I was starting out.

Now, let's say you get the Story Editor on the phone. What do you do? Make sure you have SOMETHING to say. Not just "uh ... I'm a Writer ... want to be a Writer ... and I was wondering if ... uhm ..." That ain't going to fly. Rehearse how you are going to start the conversation. And I would start by saying that you are interested in her series and would love to know what the guidelines are for submissions.

Don't try to submit over the phone, most people do that and you don't want to fall into that area. Listen to what the person has to say and say. "Okay, let me see what I can do. Is it all right if I send it directly to you?" Chances are, they will say "Yes." Now, of course, you would have sent it to her office anyway, but now you can enclose a little note on it about your previous discussion and, more importantly, put the words "Requested material" on the envelope. That will usually get it right to the desk. But remember, the important thing is to be polite and professional on the phone. Don't sound desperate. And don't try to hang on the phone longer than is needed to get the info you want.

Then, after you have sent your script, wait a couple of weeks, and call to see if she got it and everything's okay. Then ... in my opinion, forget about it. Don't beat a dead horse. It doesn't mean that you got rejected, but it could. And it doesn't mean that you haven't been read, you might not have been. But beyond that point, it becomes annoying and your phone call won't be accepted. However, if later on (much later) you write a spec script which you think is much better, you have every right to call and say "Throw the other spec away! This one is much better and I'm sending it right over!"

Does the phone call work? It has. It worked for me. Doesn't mean it will or won't for you. Keep in mind that the odds in this business are always against you, but you only need them to fall in your favor once or twice to make a difference.

Number one rule, though: Remember that you are a professional. Treat others that way and, more importantly, treat yourself that way.

You mentioned panels and seminars. Are they really important?

Absolutely. If you are in Los Angeles, you should go to as many of these as you can. If you are not in Los Angeles (yet), you should get as many first person interviews with people in the business as you can, whether it be in books, articles or documentaries. Go to local film festivals, attend the panels. Take advantage of the growing number of genre conventions, the Comic Conventions and such. They all have panels on filmmaking and the industry. And most of them bring in professionals to speak. The more you know, the better off you are.

As to the Seminars, this is a great opportunity for you to meet and interact with the people that you will be working with. No, not the people on the panel (they won't be as accessible), but the people next to you. The other people in the audience have their own aspirations and you'll be surprised how many of them you come in contact with later on. The girl next to you will be an Agent; the guy with the funny hat will be a

Showrunner one day. The person who is eating the crackers is a Studio Executive in the making. And they are thinking that you are the next Oscar winning Writer. If you continue to go to Seminars, you'll run into a few of the people again. Get to know them.

As far as the people on the panels, you'll be able to ask questions and get information. But one thing you'll notice; many times the people on the stage will disagree with each other. It can be confusing, but, again, this is such an individual business where each experience is unique. What I suggested before is that you take notes on what each person is looking for in a script. More than that, when you have the names of the people you will be listening to, devote at least a full page to each name. As they speak, or when they answer questions, make notes under that person's name. Again, this is research that is necessary.

Keep a file on these people, even if they seem to drop off the face of the earth. Just because Joe Rutabaga isn't running a show right now doesn't mean that he won't be in the future. And, it certainly doesn't mean that his information is any less valid. Start a database on these people so you can easily reference them by name or keyword.

To find the best seminars, look in the trade magazines or, better, go by word of mouth. As you network with people, you will hear them talk about the seminars that helped them. Learn to look for names of Writers on films or series that you like. Search for panels and seminars where they will be speaking. If it seems like something that would benefit you, try to attend.

And, again, the Comic Conventions. Take a camera and a notepad. The notepad is for obvious reasons. The camera, well, you'll figure that out on your first day.

It seems impossible to break in. And you have to do a lot of work just to get rejected.

Jeez, have I made it seem that dark?

Okay, the fact that you have to keep writing specs is a, well, fact. So, yes, you have to keep cranking them out.

But let me give a few words of encouragement about the process …

… hold on … I know I have some here …

… still looking … don't go away…

Ah! Found them. Right under my "Agents are easy to get" booklet.

Of course you have to do a lot of work! As was once said about professional baseball "If it was easy, everyone would be doing it." We are talking about a career here, not a fly-by-night quick way of making a few bucks. Any career worth its salt takes a huge investment effort. Except, perhaps, a career in actually making salt. Seems like a self-fulfilling effort there.

Okay. Seriously. Yes, it is extremely difficult. The odds are against you. Of the thousands of aspiring

Writers out there, the vast majority of them will never sell anything. Most of them will end up in another line of work. And even of those who do manage to make a sale, the majority of those will have a career of less than two to five years. But if all that scares you, then you should leave this book on the table and slowly back away (obviously if you're reading this as an e-book, don't leave your device on the table, 'kay?). If you think you're not up to the challenge, then you are most likely correct.

Still here? Okay. So what do you have to do to break in? Some of this is going to be touching upon things I've already mentioned.

First thing is to get as much information as possible on the business. And I mean REAL information. Not soft-pedaled optimism that many instructors and books will give you. The more informed you are about the reality, the better prepared you are for the task. But to find the answer to this you can't ask the people who are trying to break in. You have to find out what the people who are hiring are looking for. When I've spoken at seminars, I always get asked what it would take to get me to hire someone. And I have a very simple answer: "Make my life easier."

And that's really what you are trying to get across to the Showrunner. "I can make your life easier by writing great scripts with quick turnaround and no major rewrites."

Showrunners LOVE to find those people. Usually, those people aren't beginners. They are people who have some knowledge of the system. But, wait, all hope is not lost for the beginner because the other thing is that many Showrunners want to be is a mentor. They want to feel as if they are helping someone along or shaping someone's talent. They want to be able to say "I found her." Ego driven? For the most part, but for your purposes, who cares?

If your script makes it to the office, it will probably sit in a stack of scripts from other hopefuls. But one of two things will happen to those scripts—they will all be read, or discarded. If they are all read, and you have what they want, you will be called in. If they are discarded, then no one knows you were in there, and so you keep submitting. (My rule of thumb is to keep submitting until someone says "go away." And even then …)

Now, let's say that your script was read and you weren't brought in. Chances are no one is going to write your name down in a black list. In fact, they probably won't even remember your name. Which means … you can submit another script later. You can't destroy your career until you have one.

Perseverance is really the key and you've heard that so many times. The cool thing about this business is that you never know when it can hit. I know people who have been at this a long time and are still at it. I know others who have written only five spec scripts and broken in. I know people who have had years of training and are still working at it, others have had no training and work all the time. What I'm getting at is that there are a huge number of intangibles and, believe it or not, they all work in your favor. In little ways, yes, but they still do. You just have to recognize them and exploit them.

The most important thing you have going for you now as a beginner is that you are having fun. Sounds sappy, but you won't realize how important that is until you have been doing this for a few years.

Is getting a job as a Writer's Assistant or Script Coordinator a good way into the business? When's the best time to try and get those jobs?

Getting Writer's assistant and script coordinator jobs are, I think, harder to get than writing assignments. I have hired them, yes, and I've been on other productions where they were brought in by the studio from a "pool." Almost all of the positions are filled by referral and recommendation, which underlines the networking you have to do. But I would say that you should start sending your resumé as soon as the Exec Producer is in her office, but also to the office manager, if there is one, at the production companies.

A question I get asked a lot is whether being an assistant leads to being a Writer. Well, yes and no. Yes, because you are able to watch the workings of a staff and get involved in the process. This sets you up in a much better position later on when that experience comes into play while looking for a job or assignment.

But as far as being promoted into the staff of that particular show, well, a provisional maybe with an ambiguous slant. Yes, it has happened. But when we hire an assistant we really want an assistant. Not someone who is lurking around waiting for the opportunity to become a Writer. We don't want to be asked if we will read someone's script all the time. We've got a show to do and we want everyone to do their job.

Sounds depressing, eh? Not completely. What you want is to eventually have the Producer ask YOU if you have a script to read. And how to do that? First thing you have to do is let the people there know that you are working toward being a Writer and you are there to learn. That shows the people that you will take more than just a business interest (a 9-to-5 interest) in what is going on. It shows a dedication.

And you should ask questions every now and then. Not simple questions like "How many pages for act one?" but things dealing with specific scripts and plots that intrigue you. "In that first script, you had Jon-Jon avoid the water. Water works perfectly, but how'd you come up with that?" And these questions should not be blowing smoke, they should be genuine. Take my word for it, you will develop a relationship with your boss that will become more open. Hopefully it will lead to that all important question "So, have you written anything? Let me look at it." That's great when it happens, but don't rely on it. First and foremost, your job is the work you were hired for. Remember that.

○ ○ ○

Anecdote Time: I was producing a series for CBS a while back. The studio brought a series of people through my office in order to get me an assistant. I asked them all what they wanted to be when they grew up (tough question since I still don't have an answer for it). I weeded out the ones that didn't say "Writer." I finally settled on this one woman. We had a good working relationship and she never pushed a script on me. But I could tell she knew her stuff.

Pages fly off the calendar and one day she asks for a day off. I ask her if everything is okay. She says that she has a pitch meeting at a series. I tell her that it's okay and she takes the day off. A week later, I find out she got the assignment. I was happy for her. Then ... a few weeks later, she asks for another day off. I ask her why ... same answer. She has a pitch meeting. She goes ... and gets the assignment. Hmmm ... Then, yet again, she asks for a day off for a pitch. I say to her "Are you getting these meetings off a spec?" She says that she is. I tell her that I want to read the spec. She hands it to me. I read it.

Next day, I call her into my office and tell her that she wrote the script better than I could have done it (no lie, no fluff, she really did.) Then I tell her that if she gets one more assignment, she's fired. She gets very upset and I tell her that she doesn't understand. If she sells one more script, she's a *Writer*. Why the heck is she working for me?

A week later, she comes into my office with a big grin and says "You're going to have to fire me."

Since then, she has gone on to work on several series. I've hired her on another show as well. She has a full and continuing career as a Writer.

Now, I can also tell you about the assistant I had who never let anyone forget he was really a "Writer." He ended up getting himself fired and being barred from the studio. But, hey, let's learn from the positives.

So, it can be done, but you have to play the cards right.

Would it be easier to break in by writing a spec pilot and selling that to the networks? Would the network assign a Showrunner to me to actually run my show?

I have run into a few of Writers who think that the easiest way to break in is to create and produce their own series (I've run into more Actors who think that's the "easy" path to becoming a working Actor, but that's another story). The simple answer is, no, it isn't easy. It isn't even a remote consideration. It's like saying that I want to be a Hotel Manager (I don't know why you would say that, but follow me on the analogy) and, in order to get that job, I'll build a hotel first then hire myself.

But let me go on and answer the last part of the question; about the newbie being attached to a Showrunner. That has happened, it kind of happened to me (although I was already a Story Editor by then, I was unknown in the pilot arenas). I had an idea that Columbia wanted to do, so they attached a Show-running team they had under contract to shepherd the project through and lend their credible names to the project. With that, I sold an idea to ABC (never written, only paid for as it turned out) and another idea to CBS (which is another story I'll get to in a moment).

That was back in the early '90s when the studios were more apt to have many Showrunners under actual contracts and pay them to develop and produce series. These are called "overall deals." Those people would have to justify their overall deals by selling pilots. If they couldn't sell anything, the studios tried to justify the paychecks by having them shepherd projects that weren't necessarily theirs. Did this cause some resentment among the Showrunners involved? I'm sure it did in many cases.

I had sold the idea to ABC based on the concept. But the CBS case was different. I had gotten a meeting to pitch the idea that I eventually sold to ABC. Before I left the meeting, the Studio Executive asked me if I had any samples of a two hour piece, in case they wanted to do a two hour pilot. Truth is, they wanted to see if I was any good or not. I left a spec screenplay I had written, the first spec I had ever written called "Harry O'Fell and the Day Hell Froze Over." Two days later I got a call from Columbia asking if I was interesting in optioning that screenplay (selling Columbia the rights to it). Turns out the Network Executive at CBS read the screenplay, really loved it, and wanted to turn it into a series.

So in the first case, the concept sold to ABC, Showrunners were assigned to me because I was an unknown in the pilot arena. ABC needed some reassurance that this new guy wasn't going to screw things up. They wanted names they could trust. Columbia provided them.

In the second case, the CBS pilot, I sold a series based on the "Harry O'Fell" spec screenplay I had left to read. Because I was working with Columbia, the same Showrunners were assigned to me.

Now, the caveats and current realities. First of all, even though I wasn't known in the pilot arena, I was still known. It was easy to look my name up and find my credits and, by then, I had worked as staff on five series and written freelance for a couple more.

Secondly, the days of the studios loading up on Showrunners and not knowing what to do with them are long gone. I did all this, not necessarily when dinosaurs ruled the earth, but let's say when mammals were just filling the abandoned niches left by their demise.

So, now to the question of whether, these days, it is worth it to write a spec pilot. I say yes, and here's my reasoning.

First, get the idea of selling the thing out of your mind. That's the least likely thing that's going to happen. The conventional logic for TV is to write spec episodes of existing series. If you are starting out, you should ALWAYS be writing spec scripts, so writing specs of existing series are a given: Yes, write them. However, I also recommend writing pilot scripts for the following reasons:

1. As of this writing, Studios and Showrunners are more open than ever to reading original material in order to judge writing. Spec episodes of series are still strong and, as I said, you should be writing them. But they will also read pilots and screenplays.

2. If you write the pilot as an open ended screenplay (meaning a two hour pilot), then you have a screenplay to shop as well (this takes careful crafting, they are NOT the same).

3. When you are established later on, you can always pull out the old pilot, brush it off, and shop it around.

4. And … this is the explosive answer … yes, there is a chance to sell that pilot.

At this point, all newbies have ignored #1, #2 and #3, and are focusing on #4. That's the horse before the cart. I made it last on the list because it is the most unlikely scenario and something you should NOT concentrate on. These days, it isn't as simple as just writing a pilot. With the new paradigm of serialized storytelling, you have to write an entire bible, treatment, episode arcs and more just to get a chance to be rejected. If it happens, great, it happens. But do NOT waste energy trying to sell a pilot at the beginning of your career. Beginning? Heck, you don't have a career. Concentrate on starting that first.

I had to mention it, though, because it is still possible. I know this because the networks and studios have been asking to see spec pilots more and more (this has to do with economics; it means that the studios and networks don't have to pay to develop them) and I've had a couple of studios ask if I'd be interested in shepherding a new series because it was written by "unknowns" (their word, not mine, so I don't know how "unknown" these people are).

So the short answer (too late!) is that the spec pilot gives you the most options. But it should be first and foremost a spec sample of your work. Don't waste too much time and energy trying to sell it, USE it to get your career going.

Is it easier to sell a spec screenplay than get a TV job?

As a complete unknown, yes, it is relatively easier to sell a feature than a series. I had mentioned this earlier in the "dark chapter" about moving to Los Angeles.

The reason goes back to that adage that the Feature World buys scripts; the TV world buys Writers. You can be a first time Writer and sell a feature because, as far as the production company is concerned, you have already done your job. The script is there, they can look at it and know it's good. And they don't have to deal with you anymore. They buy the script, give you the required WGA rewrite, then bye-bye.

But in Television, it's quite different. We don't buy scripts. We hire Writers and we develop the scripts with them. Pitching the right story is only half the job with us. We want to know that you can develop the story and (most important) that you are good to work with. We may hire a Writer even after we have shot down all his pitch ideas. If we know he's good, and we have a story we want to tell, we will hire him and give him the story. But to do that, we have to be sure that the Writer can produce the script in the time we need (not much) and the quality we require (more than most think).

For a series, even more so. The studios and networks have to be positive that they are working with someone who understands the business and the pressure. And it's an ongoing thing 24/7.

Even with Writers who have some staff experience, if they haven't run a show yet, and they are lucky enough to sell a series, they will be assigned a Showrunner from the studios overall deal list. As I mentioned, that happened to me in 1991. I had two pilots, one for ABC and one for CBS. And the highest position I had held at that time was as a Story Editor. Too low to run a show, but just high enough to show up on the studio radar. But the studio had to assign a Showrunner to me to get the networks to sign off on the pilots.

Your best bet is to write your project as a feature. If there is a possible TV series in there, and it has a bit of success, I can guarantee you that discussions about how to take it into a series will follow.

I've got a great idea for a series, I've written a pilot and several episodes. Where do I sell it?

Well what you've done, while admirable, just isn't the way it is done. At least not the way you're thinking.

Okay, a quick brief on how creating your own series happens. And, mind you, this is the theoretical way it usually happens.

First, you move to Los Angeles (see previous "dark chapter") and learn the ins and outs of the business. You network and go to seminars. You write many spec scripts, not to sell them, but to show people your ability and skill as a Writer. Eventually, you might get an assignment. Then you work as a Writer for several years, building a reputation and a resumé.

This work is done as a Freelancer, but you eventually work on staff for a series. One, if it's a hit series, many, if they aren't. During this, you make contacts and you manage to convince your Agent that you are, in fact, a money maker. Your Agent (or you) gets meetings with development people and you pitch your ideas to them. They look at your resumé and realize that you have the chops to actually write. And, they know you know how to work on staff. Hopefully, you have run at least one show, so they know you can do that, too. At that point, they run your idea around to their department heads, including sales, and see if the series might have an outlet. Bypassing a lot of details, they hire you to write a pilot script based on that idea. You write a script, they give notes, you accommodate what you can and rewrite and they look at it and decide if they want to give the series a go for production. If they do, then if you have never run a series, they will bring in someone to run the series. You would be a Producer and creator of the series and work on the staff. From that point on, you and the Showrunner would develop script ideas, have them approved by the studio, and either write them or hire them out to be written.

Okay, I have *really* simplified the process. Back to the situation you posed in your question, the problem is twofold. One, you don't have the credits to back you up. So you can forget the idea of being the Showrunner on the series.

Running a television series is more than just coming up with script ideas and it takes a <u>lot</u> of experience to do well. So the person in charge, whether you like it or not, will be the Showrunner who will be brought in.

Second problem is that you have set so much in stone already. You have not just written a pilot, you have written a series. And the studio, the network, the Showrunner will all want to have their say in what gets produced. They will all have their take on what your series is all about. I know, you're thinking that you're the one who would know since you created it. That's not the way that Hollywood looks at it. Until you have the clout of the top show creators in Hollywood, you aren't going to call all the shots. So instead of writing episodes, you write your proposed story arcs, perhaps eight to ten paragraphs of individual stories, each one to be an episode. Or, if you're idea is really ambitious, you write out a treatment for the entire first and second season as if they were movies. Yes, it's still a lot set in stone, but it's still able to move and breathe a bit. It gives you more of a handle on your characters and stories without the appearance of locking them in.

Sure, you want to believe that it's the overall story that counts. Obviously, if they buy the series, you'll let them do anything with the scripts you wrote. And you are, logically, right. But don't play to logic. Play to the appearance your series proposal might have. In a game of inches, you don't want to spook them in any way.

This is all without addressing the fact that you don't have an Agent with the clout to get you into the meetings and introduce you to the people you need to meet.

So what can you do with all your hard work? Well, first of all, feel proud about yourself. Most people talk a good story, but rarely take the time to actually write one. Everybody has a great idea for a new series ... and never take the time to actually write a script. Kudos to you for that.

But here's what I would suggest. You need to create a "presentation package" for your series. Hollywood is always anxious to read pilot scripts, so you're ahead there. But one of the areas that a lot of Writers (pro and amateur) fall down on is when they are in the meeting and one of the execs says "great premise. So tell me what episode seven would be about." What they are asking is an example of the week to week kind of stories. You'd be surprised how many Writers don't take the time to figure that out. If you have, in fact, written extra episodes, you would be able to answer this easily. Just don't pull out the already-written scripts (or mention that you already wrote them).

So, for this package, you should write an introduction for the series (one page, one paragraph, quick and to the meat of what makes this series different). Then a treatment for the series, where you go into detail about the characters and their relationships. Your pilot script next, you already have that. Then prepare a synopsis of all your episodes. One paragraph each, they should read slightly better than a *TV Guide* blurb. Number them. But title them as "Possible episodes."

DO NOT let them know that you have them all written out, no matter how tempting it is. Okay, you might say you wrote one extra script or two just to get the feel of the series, but don't scare them by saying you have the first two seasons already written out. After you get the deal, you can mention it. But if you've gotten this far, you don't need to show them your additional writing (and, possibly, additional problems).

Now some series presentations include a sizzle reel, or a trailer, to show what the series would be about. DON'T DO THIS! At least not unless you are really really really really really good at filmmaking. In other words, unless you already have an experienced career. I know how tempting this is. I see people doing it all the time. I have yet to see one amateur sizzle reel or trailer for a series that didn't look like a well intentioned home movie.

Anyway, once your presentation is ready to go, you go … well, that's the question, isn't it? And if it was a simple thing, like just putting in an employment application, there wouldn't be a profitable business in "How To" books for Television, would there?

You make a list. Several lists, as a matter of fact. And you have to understand you have already jumped the gun here, so you're having to play catch-up. You need an Agent to take your work around, or a Manager to introduce you to people. You need to get yourself known in the production offices of various companies.

Although they have been much derided, I would suggest you concentrate on the Agents list first. Keeping in mind that you need to develop yourself as a Writer, not just someone who wrote a pilot.

You can also try making phone calls to the development people of the various studios. Sometimes, lightning strikes. Someone might pick up your proposal and give it a read.

If you decide to mail your work blind to people, make sure that you address it to a specific person and keep your cover letter to a minimum. Don't be too arrogant (saying you have the best series that has ever been conceived is arrogant) and don't say that you are a beginning Writer who wants to get into the business. Keep it professional. "Enclosed is a project I have been working on. I think you'll find it interesting. Thank you for your time and enjoy." or something like that. That's really all you need. The next page should be your intro page. And, hopefully, that will be compelling enough to make them read more.

What do I do when I get a pitch meeting for a possible episode assignment?

In this, we are talking about the idea that you have managed to get a meeting set to go in and pitch ideas for an assignment to write one episode of an existing TV series (not selling a pilot and series). This is where you start as far as the business is concerned. You already have the meeting, so that's a big step in itself.

The first thing and the most important thing is to be PROFESSIONAL. I cannot stress this enough.

You might have figured out that this is a big deal with me. Not just me, but with the business because it IS a business. Be professional. You are respectful, but you expect respect. You are a contributor. You are someone who counts, otherwise you wouldn't be in this meeting. And, you have a right to say NO to anything that really bothers you. At the same time, you are expected to be a team player and work within the bounds set. You are expected to give 110% in your efforts. And if there is a problem, you are expected to be professional in how you handle it.

1. Basics:

Before you go to the meeting, get familiar with the series. If you can, watch the show on TV, online, or get DVDs of some of the episodes. More importantly, get scripts that they have produced. Do NOT be afraid to ask for these. They are tools for your pitch and all series will provide them. Most do it without even asking. Hopefully they will provide you with a series "bible" if they have one. A "bible" for a series is the complete outline of the series, the characters, the stories arcs, almost everything there is to know about the series. Even better, if they have an episode list of stories already done or in the works, get that, too. Again, don't be afraid to ask for all of these. They may have them, they may not.

In the rare case that you might know someone who has already gone into this office to pitch, talk to him and get the feel of what you are walking into.

Keep in mind that your friend will have his own filters and impressions that might bias things. And, of course, that the friend might not really be a friend and want sabotage you. Take the info and put it into the back of your mind for reference, don't use it to pre-judge anything.

There is no rule on what to expect when you walk into the room. Hopefully, it will be a friendly room (it usually is). But be prepared for anything. The Showrunner or a Producer may be in the room. Many, many times you will run into people who are on their first staff jobs as Writers. There are times when their egos will come into play. Keep in mind they have the job you want. They know that. So there might be a little political biting going on. Ignore it. Focus on what you are there to do.

Don't go in with ten ideas. Go in with no more than five. I really recommend three, but I have cheated on occasion. Make sure that you have those ideas well thought out. The guest starring characters, how the main characters react and interact with them. The beginning, middle and end of the story including your B plot as well as how it affects the A plot. Know your stories so well you can answer any question thrown at you. And, if for some reason you can't answer the question, turn it into a positive by brainstorming in the room. Move quick, react quicker. Welcome the question, don't dread it. The more questions they ask in the room, the more they are trying to move you toward what they need. And they wouldn't do that if they weren't interested in working with you.

Remember that your primary purpose in the story is to service the regular characters. Not the new, nifty character that you hope they will spin-off into a series. Everything has to be reflected on the main characters. Keep in mind that the characters are all different and have different attitudes. Make sure you throw those differences in now and then. "Claudia and Tom have to go get the child from the mother, which will be really interesting because, you know, she was adopted herself and Tom doesn't understand it."

Keep your ideas within budget. This will take some finesse as most Freelancers aren't aware of budget issues. Watching the series will give you some idea, but be prepared to hear that your idea is beyond their budget. When you do hear this, keep in mind that they are talking about something that will be hard to visualize, so have a back-up idea ready. Not another story idea, but another way to get your story point across. There is always a cheaper alternative. Have it ready as a back-up.

Have your ideas on paper for your reference. More on that in a moment.

Remember that different series rely on different presentation styles. I personally believe it's all about characters, no matter whether you are doing an eight hour dramatic series or an episodic action adventure comedy. But the focus is different. Remember that one, for example, might be more visual and appeal to more common denominators; action, sex, humor. Doesn't mean you can be a hack, but it does mean you have to keep those things in mind when you write. For example, you can have two characters discussing their character differences at a romantic dinner or in a hot tub. Which one do you think will sell better? It doesn't change what the discussion is, just the presentation.

If you feel the series is beneath you, don't take the meeting. "I would never write for THAT show" is a common phrase among new Writers. Aside from being arrogant, it belies the truth. If that show offers you a job, 99% of the people will jump at the chance. If you're smart, you'll still write the best possible episode for that series. Along those lines, don't think that any series is easy to write. "How difficult can it be?" is another often heard phrase. Well, damn difficult. Don't get cocky, don't get arrogant. Want the job or don't waste anyone's time.

2. Styles:

There are many different ways to approach your pitch. The second hardest part for me is just the first couple of lines. The transition from the pleasant talk to the pitch itself. Sometimes, it's just good enough to say "okay, let's get into it. My first idea …"

When you actually pitch the idea, again, there are different ways to do it. One way is to give the logline; a quick description of the core point of the episode. It's straightforward and antiseptic. It relies on the

Producers being able to see the consequences of the idea and play it out along their series lines. The logline should be somewhere around three to six lines long. Nothing more involved than that at the moment. If they don't throw the idea out completely, you are then free to go into detail.

Another way is to use a hook. "What would happen if …" for example. You want to present them with a scenario that BEGS to be told. You might lay the groundwork for your hook by saying "As I understand it, Character B is really in love with Character D. So, what would happen if …"

Yet another way is to use a teaser set-up. "We open the episode on a dark road in the middle of a thunderstorm …" You will tell, basically, the teaser. Remember that the teaser to any episode is, really, a hook. If done well, it leaves the audience wanting more, wanting an explanation, wanting to see how their characters will respond. After you get to the "ooh, yeah!" moment, you can stop and say "Okay, now what's really happened is …"

3. "Oooh Yeah!"

It's actually a George Carlin term. It's that moment that everyone in the room goes "ooh, yeah!" At that moment, they got it. And you got them.

4. Before You Walk In

This starts before you get into your car. Go over all your ideas. Read them out loud without pitching them. Read them as they are written on your pages. This serves two purposes: One, it gets you up to speed on your material. And, two, it works the kinks out of your voice. And, yes, this is something to pay attention to. You want your voice to be comfortable and not strained. Any one of you who were actors knows exactly what I am talking about and the importance of vocal exercise in any presentation.

If you have a regiment of doing a physical workout, do it. Loosen up. Feel good.

Depending on the time of day, eat whatever is your norm but don't over-drink. This is IMPORTANT. You don't want to notice that tingling in your bladder when in the pitch. Hold off on drinking a lot until you get there. Chances are they will ask if you want anything to drink. At that point tell them you want some water. Then, don't drink it until you are actually heading into the pitch room. The water isn't to refresh your thirst, it is to keep your throat from being too dry.

Take a small notepad or tablet, a pen, at least two copies of your pages and a voice recorder (more on this in a bit).

Dress comfortably. Don't overdress. If you're a guy, wear casual slacks or nice jeans and a nice shirt. If you are female, you can wear slacks, nice jeans, a nice dress, whatever. For both, don't try to impress with your wardrobe. That means don't show off how wealthy you are or how sexy you are. That's not what this meeting is about and it's distracting. There will be more on this later on.

When you are on your way in your car, repeat your pitches, again, out loud. You can't read this time, so it will reinforce what things stood out for you in your stories. And you will also discover certain turns of phrase that will more than help you in your pitch. Turn the radio off, stay focused. Oh, and keep your eyes on the road; driving safely is, still, your main function.

When you are in the waiting room, take out one of the copies of your pages and go through them again (not out loud this time). And, here's something that is also important; mark up your pages. Take a pen (hopefully you brought one with you) and MARK THE PAGES. Make notes in the margins, even if you don't have anything to note. Just harmless things. Why? Read on.

Be careful what you say to anyone. You never know who you are talking to or who might overhear you. I was once heading into a casting session when I heard an Actor talking to another Actor about the scene he had to read from one of our scripts. He told the other Actor "I could do this in my sleep" while waving the pages. He didn't notice me so when he got into the room, he didn't react to me being the one he was auditioning for. Fortunately, this guy was not real good, so it cleared my conscience. But when he was done, he asked if there was another way I wanted to see it done. I said "How about in your sleep?" He froze. He apologized and we had a laugh over it, but it's a good lesson to learn.

Now, IF you are made to wait (and you will be) only you will know your tolerance level of how long you are kept waiting. I have a few rules of my own, but they don't apply to everyone else. I can be a little more intolerant and stand on righteous indignation, a beginning Writer can't. Just understand that you will have to wait longer than you expected. Hopefully you will at least get an apology.

5. In the Room

You will be introduced to everyone in the room. Try to remember everyone's name. If not, certainly remember their titles. And keep in mind that EVERYONE in that room is important. Do NOT neglect anyone in your pitch. The assistant is just as important as the Executive Producer as far as you are concerned. And, please, if you miss the introductions, or if you are just told "here's the gang," do NOT assume that the only woman in the room is an assistant. In my many, many experiences in pitch sessions, I have seen this happen over and over, from men *and* women.

Don't meander around. There will be a seat for you, sit in it immediately.

Keep in mind that this is not JUST to hear your ideas. The people in the room want to get a sense of who you are. Unlike features, where the Writer writes a script and the production doesn't have to deal with them, Television develops WITH the Writer. They have to work with you, so they want to know what you are like. Do you listen? Are you overbearing? Are you opinionated? Are you humorous? Are you quiet? They want to get an idea of what it will be like working with you. How much does this play in your hiring? It means a lot. Whether it's fair or not, it is very true that the room will be more forgiving to a Writer if they enjoy having her around.

Make sure your energy is up. Many staffs are very quick in their thoughts and reactions, they have worked together, they have a shorthand they speak with each other. They have "in" jokes that they all know. Ignore the jokes, you'll only look foolish trying to participate. But be quick to adapt to changing situations. One of the best things that can happen is when the staff starts to rewrite your story in the room. Best things, you say? Doesn't that mean that my story is deficient? No, quite the opposite. It means that it caught their attention. It means that the story has affected them and they are already trying to make it fit into their series. If this happens (and you want the job) don't stop them and say "Hey, this is MY idea and it doesn't change!" That's the best way to lose an assignment. No, what you want to do is join in. This is your chance to actually be a part of the staff. And, more than that, it's your chance to shine as a team player. Go with it.

There will come a time when you are beginning a pitch and before you get three words out, someone will say "We're not going to do those kinds of stories" or "we're already doing that." If that happens, don't push it UNLESS you haven't yet reached the meat of the story. My suggestion is to stop your pitch and go immediately to the logline version of the story. If all you've mentioned is the window dressing, make sure they understand that it isn't what the story is about. But if they say it again after hearing your explanation, drop it and move on. If this happens to ALL your ideas, don't become desperate. Admit that you don't have anything else to present at the moment, but that you have some things to think about. Say you'd like to come back in again. Then thank them.

If it is allowed, bring a voice recorder and record the meeting. This is for your protection and theirs. If the Producer or Executive is smart, she will start with a disclaimer that says that there are other ideas in the works that may have similarities to your ideas, that you should understand that many ideas have yet to be discussed internally, etc. That's for their protection so you don't try to sue them when you see something familiar later on. Your protection is that if they say you have a job, then renege on it later, you have proof. But what you tell them is that you want to make sure you get everything because you might have a great idea in the room that you'll forget about later. You want to make sure you get it recorded. If the room says that they are uncomfortable with a recorder, don't argue, but make sure you stay focused on the idea of taking notes. Say that you would still like to take notes just in case and pull out your pen and pad.

As you might have picked up on, I earlier wrote the first few lines to start the pitch was the "second hardest" part of the meeting. You might have logged that in your mind as "so, what's the hardest part?" Simple. The second hardest part is how to start your pitch. The hardest part is how to STOP.

Yeah, you read that correctly. And most people don't think about it. You just stop when you finish your pitch, right? Sure. If you can.

When you reach the end of your pitch, here's what is most likely to happen.

Silence.

Now that silence is probably a result of them assessing what you said or, in many cases, waiting for the boss to speak first, to see how she feels so they'll know how they feel about your pitch.

But to you … the few seconds of silence are going to grow exponentially until it seems like minutes on end of them just staring at you. As if they are still waiting for you to hook them. As if they still don't quite get what you are pitching. That silence is going to be a monster because we, as human beings, hate silence. It makes us uncomfortable and it's a void that has to be filled. So you will be urged to fill it. You might start to fumble through things, repeating stuff you've already mentioned, or trying to underline things you think they missed.

Don't do that. When you are finished, end it. And make them know that they burden of the silence is upon them, not you. It's their turn to speak and react.

How you do that is up to you. You definitely have to have your ending in mind and stick to it. But you also need to make sure they understand when you are done and you've turned the floor over to them. You could say something as simple as "And that's that." Then sit back in your chair and wait. Interestingly enough, it's the sitting back in the chair that is the actual signal. For me, I have the water they offered me and I start drinking. With that, I've excused myself from the burden of silence. In psychological terms, I've forced the burden of silence onto them. Come up with something that works for you, something that definitively draws the curtain on the pitch, brings the houselights up, and lets them know the discussion can begin.

6. Intangibles

Now, having said how you need to project an image of being enjoyable, don't suck up. Don't try to be chummy with the room. Follow their lead. Many times, the room will just want to get down to business. Other times, they will chatter and will want to talk a bit. Don't be thrown off either way. One of the things I have been accused of by my staff is that I tend to go off on tangents and chat a bit. My Co-Exec Producer on my last show made it a habit of sitting slightly behind the Freelancer so that she could glare at me when I was taking too much time. But that's not for you to worry about, just go with the flow. At a certain point, you'll feel when the room is ready.

Keep in mind what the room has already been through. Many times, the room has seen other Writers that day. They are probably tired. They are probably frustrated. They are DESPERATELY trying to find someone to fulfill the open slots so they can get back to their own jobs. Be that person.

Don't stay any longer than is necessary. If possible, end the meeting yourself. Finish your pitches, see if there is anything else they would like to hear, then thank them and go.

Someone will inevitably ask you if you have something to leave behind, outlines or paragraphs of the episodes you just pitched. You do have those, but do you leave them or not? Well, that depends on what you learned in the meeting and what your pitches evolved into.

If the pitch goes exactly as you planned it and nothing was changed during the discussion, then, sure, leave the pages. But it's very likely that things will not go as you planned and that your stories will change as they offer their input.

It's very possible that you will also hear things in the meeting that you realize you put in your pages, things that that they shouldn't see. For example, in *Xena*, we made a clear distinction between Magic and Powers. We didn't have Magic, but gods had Powers. It may sound slight to you, but it was an important difference to us. We also took exception to being called a "swords and sorcery" series as we felt it misrepresented what we were really doing. In your pages, you suddenly realize that you played up Ares using his magic to defeat Xena or started a page by saying "The staple in most sword and sorcery series ..." You are completely innocent and you meant no offense. However, you don't feel comfortable leaving those pages.

Also, there are times when someone will mention something in the meeting and you, being smart, seize on it and run with it, adding it to your pitch as if it was always a part of it. But it isn't in your pages. So what do you do then?

Remember when I told you to take two copies of your pitches and mark one of them up? Well, first, you make a judgment call. The Producers will understand that things got changed in the meeting, but are there things that you really think might hurt your chances? Did you run with an idea spontaneously that, though you seamlessly added it in as if it was always your intent, isn't in your written pitch? If not, and you feel comfortable with what you've written, just pull out the clean copy and leave it with them. If so, if it's not representative of what happened in the room, pull out the marked copy and say something like "My pages are so marked up right now, let me just send you a copy as soon as I get home."

Do not expect to be told you sold an idea in the room. The staff needs to talk about it. Yes, it's possible that the Showrunner will tell you that you did, but more likely you'll walk out with a polite "Thank you for coming in. We'll be in touch."

Before you leave the office, take a moment to thank the assistant for the water or whatever.

Establish communication with that person. Get their name and remember it. Don't linger.

7. After the Meeting

When you get home, write a journal entry about the meeting. List the names of the people there, who they were, what their titles were. List the episodes you pitched and their reactions in your database. You want to make a log of what happened so that you can reference it for the next meeting and, also, refer to it if one of these people moves onto another show. Once you have done that ... let it go. I can tell you right now, you are going to obsess about what could have or couldn't have happened in that meeting, how you screwed up, how you failed, and so on, and so on.

Worse, you might think the meeting went incredibly well and that a contract is being fashioned for you even as you walk to your car. Your *old* car; might as well start shopping for a hot new model now that you have a six-episode deal.... Okay, come back to reality as soon as possible. None of those things are true. Move on to your next project or meeting. Never let the last meeting carry over into the next. And, keep in mind, you will have many more meetings where you don't sell anything than ones where you do. Learn to take the rejection in stride and forget about the new car.

No one is required to call you and tell you that they turned down your ideas. Your Agent, if you have one, will do a follow up. If not, you may, after a week or so, call the assistant and ask. But only do it once.

8. Final Notes

You may or may not have gotten that assignment, but the real purpose of that meeting was for them to get a feel for you. It's very possible that you might get another meeting to pitch more ideas. If you really made a hit in the room, it's also possible they may call you in to pitch *you* one of *their* ideas. They may have already decided they want you to write a script, so they're going to give you an idea of theirs to work on. If that happens ... congratulations. You succeeded in turning the entire meeting around.

What is the expected style of dress for meetings?

I am always amused when I get an invitation for social events where the dress is specified as "business casual." I'm usually in jeans and a comfortable shirt, but I hardly think that is what they mean.

Comfortable, though, is the key. Wear what is comfortable and "respectful." You don't want to dress up, that's a sign of an amateur. You want to be casual. Wear slacks and a comfortable shirt. That's really it. My style when I'm relaxing is khakis and a safari style shirt, so that's what I wear to a meeting. Though I have been known to sport a pair of jeans every now and then.

Bill Martell, in an article he wrote for Script Secrets magazine, made mention of me in a particular context which I had never thought of, but is kind of interesting. In his article, he suggested that you have a "signature." Nothing obvious, nothing in anyone's face. But something that people will notice over time. What Bill had written about me was that I always wear a fedora. Truth is, I wear it because I look better in it and I've worn it for so long that people now *expect* me to wear it. But, he's right, people now identify me with that hat. More than that, I usually wear what is known as a "safari" or "Australian" type of pants and shirt. And somewhere in my ensemble, you will find at least one Florida State University logo.

None of that was done as a specific pitching choice, but just my casual wear. However, after a while, people manage to maintain an "image" of me based on my attire in their mind and it has stuck as a representation of me. One of the things you want to do, if you can, is to stand out without standing out. How you present yourself is the major part of that.

Be comfortable. That's the main thing you want to feel and want to project.

I have a chance to pitch at one of those five minute pitch seminars (Where you are given five minutes to pitch your idea to Studio Execs). What should I do to prepare?

I'm not sure these happen a lot these days, but addressing the question will give you some insights in the pitching process.

Many studios used to have outreach programs like this. The odds of actually selling anything are small, but it's not something you should refuse. At the least, you will meet new people to network with and have a chance to hone your pitch skills.

These are very specialized sessions. Unlike a regular pitch meeting, you aren't given a lot of time. You are also part of a "cattle call." It's a much more organized assembly line atmosphere. You have to make the best of what you've got.

Next, there is no way you can do a complete pitch in five minutes. So don't try to do it. These five minute sessions aren't intended to get a sale, it's intended to get them interested in meeting with you later. What you want to do is make them want to hear more than five minutes so that they will call you later and meet with you for an actual pitch meeting.

There is no way you can anticipate the questions you might get (though in five minutes, I'm willing to bet you won't get many). But no matter how many they ask, if any, you still have to have the answers. The only preparation for this is to know your series and characters so well that there is no way they can ask a question that you can't either answer or make up an answer for on the spot. That takes an intimate and expansive knowledge of your series. I look at it this way: To go into a half hour meeting, I have to be prepared to talk up to two hours about my series. In other words, I pretend I am on a stage at a convention, with fans asking me the most obscure of questions, and have been asked to talk about my new series idea with no time restraints.

And I'm not kidding you, I can talk for two hours about my series. Why wouldn't I? It's talking about a world I created, a world I am still creating. It's my joy and passion. I was once in a meeting for the series *Sheena*, I was meeting with some of the executives at SONY and they asked me to tell them about the series. Somewhere around the one hour mark, one of them stopped me and said they had never run into a Producer who knew more about their series than I did. Of course I would. This is my playground.

If you can do that, you'll know more than anyone will ever want to know.

But the situation I'm talking about won't allow you hours to talk. In fact, it's even more difficult. You have mere minutes to get it across. Don't rush through it and try to get all the information out. You'll only succeed in slighting everything. The outline of the pilot episode isn't important, but it's important that you know what it is (in case they ask you a direct question). You need to use your brief description of the series, and be able to pitch it in an exciting and interesting way. You need to know your main characters, but don't get too locked in on details. Don't bother going through an in depth character analysis. Tell the things that are unique and integral to your series.

Only mention your future episode ideas in regards to the pitch. In other words, something like this: "Jeremy X can read minds, but only the minds of people he's actually met. Which really comes into play in one of the future episodes I'm thinking about." That's it, no elaboration. It tells them that you have already considered future episodes and can talk about them if they want to, but don't use up your pitch time to explain to them the details. If you have a little time after the basic pitch, you can also say "We got really excited about this because the episode ideas just starting pouring out. Jeremy's father plays a part in one episode, his younger sister finds out she has the power, which is another episode we thought of." But no more than that.

See, what you want to do is get them excited enough to start asking you the questions. The reason for this is that you can use their questions to judge which aspects they are interested in and adjust accordingly, but it also shows that they are intrigued. And that is important to the sales of a series. Every promo you've ever seen for a new series is designed to intrigue the audience; they pose questions that the audience wants to know the answer to, and the only way to do that is to tune in. The executives are the same way. You have to intrigued them, not inform them. You want them to be so curious about your idea that they are willing to bring you back to answer their questions.

Remember what I've already written, about pitching? You need to have that opening line ready to go, to slide right into your pitch. In these kinds of meetings, it will usually be much more well defined. Face it, in this case, you're on the starting line waiting for the green light. When it flashes green, you start immediately.

So how do you approach it? Everyone might have their own style, but there are two that I prefer.

Inception—This is when I tell them what started me thinking about this idea. For example: "I was having lunch with a friend and I said something and he said 'When hell freezes over.' I said 'When it does, you'll owe me.' Then I started thinking … if it did, EVERYONE would owe something. So I started thinking about this guy.…" (by the way, that was an actual pitch that I sold). What I did there is started the flow by saying how this weird and unique idea came into my head.

The Teaser Pitch: In this, I actually start by describing the opening scene of the pilot. But only, ONLY, if that opening scene sets up intriguing questions. For example: "We start with a wedding; beautiful, lots of white, happy people and, of course, the couple in love. It's the reception and they are dancing away, the ring bearer, a six year old boy, trying to dance and stealing the show from the couple. Outside, we see this low slung, black BMW Z4 pull up. The valet opens the door and a pair of sexy legs step out. This is JESSICA, she's wearing white, but it contrasts her black hair and dark sunglasses. She heads inside where the happy couple are sharing their loving cup. Only a couple of people look at Jessica as she walks up and, without a pause, pulls a pistol and shoots the bride in the forehead. Pandemonium breaks out, people screaming. The groom charges her, she shoots him. She turns and shoots the best man and two other people. It's not random, she is picking her targets. She's a killer, an assassin. And she's our hero. As our hero turns to leave, she sees the little boy and raises her gun toward him....Okay, now what's happening here is …" and I go into the explanation of the pitch. The point of this is to accomplish many things at once. It intrigues them (what the HELL is going on here? She's our HERO???) and it sets the tone of the series; they get an idea of the darkness and explosiveness of each episode. And, more importantly, I try to tell it in a visual manner so they can SEE it.

You have to judge which one of these works for you (if either). And you have to be able to time it out so that you will have time to finish your pitch after your set up. This will take some practice and I suggest you do practice. Although the styles I just mentioned are ones I prefer in a regular series pitch meeting, you only have five minutes, so don't spend a lot of time on pleasantries. "Hi. Nice to meet you. Okay, this is what I have …" Get right to it.

Finally, as I said it is often hard to figure out how to begin, it is almost impossible to know when to stop. You're going to feel as if you are a train out of control, that every empty space has to be filled with dialogue. Don't fall into that trap. When you finish your pitch, STOP TALKING. End it and ask them if there are any questions. They may or may not. They may just say "Thank you" and that's it. Don't let either response rattle you. As long as you did your pitch correctly, you succeeded.

And, no matter how they respond, do NOT let your physical demeanor show your feelings. I can guarantee you, even though you know this logically, if they say anything except "We love it and want to buy it right now!" you're going to feel depressed, as if you failed. You can't let that show, you have to stand up with just as much energy as you walked in with, flash them the smile and walk out with your shoulders square, letting them know that YOU know that your pitch was a home run. Your confidence can gloss over a lot of doubts others might have.

So, recapping:

Rehearse your opening line to start the meeting.

Pitch your series idea in an intriguing and question provoking manner. If it involves outlining the pilot, only use what's necessary.

Outline your characters briefly, if possible during the pitch.

Get the idea across to them that you have thought up future episodes and, more importantly, that the series has "legs."

When you run out of things to say STOP TALKING! Don't try to fill empty space.

Walk out with the same energy and determination you walked in with.

A TV Producer of my favorite show has asked for a spec script but all I have is a spec screenplay (because I'm really not interested in TV). Should I send it or try to write a spec episodic script? And is that different from writing a feature script?

First, obviously, if you aren't really interested in TV, then don't get involved with it. But what you probably mean is that it isn't your primary focus. Someone offers you a chance to write professionally, I think you'll find the passion.

What do you know about this particular Showrunner? It's possible that this person has no problem with reading a spec screenplay. If that's the case, you may not have as much of a problem as you think.

Other than that, the same rules apply; don't spec the show you want to write for. However, if you like this show, spec it … and use the script as a sample for other shows (like no one expected me to say that). Keep in mind that people in TV don't want a one-hit wonder. This goes back to the question of your interest in TV. In other words, wanting to jump into the TV pool just to write for one series isn't very practical. If this series prompts you into getting into the TV world, that's cool. Chances are by the time you get a shot at your favorite show, it will be gone. And, as a cruel side note, people who have favorite shows are frequently the worst at pitching for them. So be careful there.

Now, as to the actual scriptwriting, here're some pointers to keep in mind when going from feature writing to TV.

There is a continuity of flow in screenplays that you don't have in most teleplays. The majority of teleplays (ignoring pay TV such as HBO or Showtime for the moment) has commercial breaks and you have to accommodate them. In screenplays, you can be more true to the natural three act structure. In TV, it's forced at best. The reason is because your script is broken up into four or five acts because of the necessary commercial breaks. And, remember, you have to write toward those breaks so that the audience doesn't changed channels during the commercials. You can't take a screenplay and just insert commercials at four or five equidistant places in the script just as you can't take a teleplay, remove all the commercial breaks, and have a full screenplay structure.

Another thing is that TV is faster paced than the screen. You have to write within a strict time period (say 43 minutes or so for a one hour episode; 90 minutes for a two hour episode). You have very little leeway to nudge it forward or back. In screenplays, the timing on the final feature is subject to less restriction. You can be 109 minutes ... or 115 minutes ... whatever amount of time is needed to best tell the story. In TV, it is the amount of time necessary to fill the time allotted.

In TV, when writing an episode of an existing series, the lead characters are already established. There is little need to explain who they are and how they came to this situation. You are able to move directly into the plot of the episode. In features, the characters are stand alone, so you have to create them on-screen for the audience. Still, in TV, you do have to explain the guest starring characters. This takes time that, in a feature, you would have the luxury to explore. In TV, you have to shortcut it using stereotype, audience assumption, reveals and blatant exposition (to be avoided if possible).

The bottom line is that features and TV serve different masters (audience versus advertisers) and have to be painted on different canvases. The best way I can say it is that feature scripts can afford to be "leisurely," TV scripts can't. In other words, Film is sitting on the rocks over Big Sur, sipping on some sauce and chilling at the awesome vibe. TV is New York, running from one station to another to catch the subway, praying that you'll hit the next train on time.

Screenplays tend to have more time to develop different character threads. Teleplays focus in on the main characters, the "A" and "B" plots, and lose or diminish the rest. At best, you might have time for some character touches. If at all possible, have the "A" and "B" unite somehow in your fourth act, preferably to add to the solution.

Again, each act break in a Television script has to bring the audience back. If it's a four act structure, the first act ends with an "Ah, hah!" The second act ends with an "Uh, oh …" the Third Act ends with a "Holy damn!"

Or, as I like to view them, the end of the first act is a major chord, with a rising fifth. The end of the second act is an inharmonic. The third act ends with a minor chord, descending. Yes, I played in the band in high school. Surprisingly, many of the Writers I've worked with have had some sort of musical background. A side note, but I find it interesting.

In TV, silence has to mean something. There is no space (or "beat") between dialogue just to service a small character moment. Aside from annoying your actors, you have to service the character but get on with it. If it is an ensemble cast, make SURE you service ALL the characters. Even if the focus is on one of the characters, the others are important, too. One way to deal with them is to give them your "B" plot while the focus takes the "A" plot.

When you write your zero draft (that's the draft no one will see, just your initial roadmap), DON'T BE AFRAID TO OVERWRITE IT. If you are aiming for a 60 page script, you might find you've overwritten it by ten to twelve pages. However, make sure you understand that those ten to twelve pages will have to come out in the end. Don't think that you have written it so incredibly well that the script just can't be cut back. It can. And if you don't do it, someone else will. Better you do it than them. For one thing, it will be less painful. For another, it shows you know what you are doing.

When you do cut the ten pages, remember that you will HAVE to make choices. There is an old adage in TV "If you love it, kill it" or, as Arthur Quiller-Couch said "Murder your darlings" (yes, he was the first one to write that in this context, look it up). Basically it means that are bound to become attached to something in the script, some turn of phrase or some really neat and clever action. And as you start cutting back and condensing, you will try to hold onto that little love as long as you can, even though you know it really isn't as important to the script as you want it to be. So the rejoinder to the old adage is "save it for the screenplay." Cut it. Kill it. Move on.

And don't try to cram ten pages into one. It won't happen. Choices have to be made, you will have to make them and massage them throughout the script so it appears as if there were never any hard choices made.

So, on the topic of condensing, how does one go about it? Cut out every other verb? Well, in the easy cases, you'll find a cute scene that doesn't really need to be in the episode (see "love" choices above). It can go and there's a page or two at one slash. But at a certain point, just cutting doesn't do it. You have to start combining. Layering things so that three scenes worth of information get condensed into one scene. If you do it right, no one will notice it. It will seem totally natural.

Keep in mind that TV doesn't have the budget or, in most cases, the scope of film.

Also, keep in mind that everyone above story editor level know all the tricks to cramming pages. Don't widen your margins or cheat your dialogue. That's a sign of being an amateur.

Homework Time!!!

Here's a bit of homework for you. Obviously you don't have to do this, it's not like the script police are going to send me your name if you don't. But I can guarantee you, if you do this homework honestly, you will be a much better Writer.

You are going to write a ten page scene. There will be five characters in the scene. You can come up with any situation you choose; locked in an elevator, buying a car, designing a new thumbtack, whatever. The scene should have a beginning, middle and end. That is to say a quick setup for the situation, interaction with the characters and they are confronted with a problem, and a resolution to the problem. The characters should all be given equal time (note: this doesn't mean equal dialogue, it means equal participation in the scene). Each character should be distinct from the others; they should each have their own attitude, their own perspective, their own emotions, and so on. Each character should interact with the other characters to resolve the problem in their own distinct ways.

Write that scene in ten pages. When you are done, go back, reread it, focus it, and write it again. And again. And keep rewriting those ten pages until they are as tight and as perfect as possible (if you haven't rewritten at least three times, you aren't trying).

Now, the test:

Rewrite it once more, only drop it to five pages and don't lose anything.

What??????

Repeat: Lose five pages. Keep everything.

Okay, now what this homework does is teach you how to condense and focus. It teaches you to use actions and innuendo to replace dialogue and exposition. It teaches you how to layer your scene so that one thing means many. Trust me, you will learn more about scene writing with this one test than you will by writing a dozen scripts. And this isn't just a great test for Writers, I recommend it for Directors and Actors, too.

For Writers, though, it has more than just an instructional purpose. It has a practical application in the production world. Especially when you are asked to rewrite your script or edit it. It will also come in handy when you have to reduce, say, your screenplay to a teleplay.

Is it easy for a first time writer to get a producing job in TV?

First, let's understand the staff positions in a TV show. The usual staff progression is:

Freelance Writer
Staff Writer
Story Editor
Producer
Supervising Producer
Co-Executive Producer
Executive Producer

Between Story Editor and Producer, you might also see Executive Story Editor or Co-Producer. Those are, more or less, half step credits. In theory, each position has specific duties and responsibilities. In reality, the titles are too often used as ego credits and negotiating ploys (a note on that later).

So how could, as you ask, a first time Writer get a Producer credit?

A Writer might have written a hit feature (or, even, a moderately successful feature). And, even though that Writer has no experience in TV, they are given a series deal and made an Executive Producer.

That has to do with the power the Writer has as a result of his success in the feature world. If it was his feature that is being turned into a TV series, he has more leverage in that regard. Usually, since the Writer doesn't have the actual experience of a TV Producer, the studio will bring in a "real" Producer to run the show in the background.

Or an Exec Producer has a favorite Writer they want to work with and makes that person a part of the deal, bringing him in as a Producer when he really isn't qualified.

A Writer might retain the rights to a project that the studio wants, such as a novel or the rights to a person's true story. He can make his own deal and call his own title.

Or you're the studio president's boyfriend.

In other words, it's a vanity credit that can often be given for reasons that have little to do with actual producing.

So let's forget all the favoritism clauses and talk about the credits as they are intended to be, with duties and responsibilities.

Using that as the base, no, a Writer cannot be promoted directly into Producer. The reason is because the duty of a Writer is to write. The duties of a Producer are only partly writing. You are now entering the realm of practical production, which takes a whole new set of skills. Many of which can be book-taught, but most of which come at the hand of experience. And if experience is a necessary requirement, you aren't going to have the qualifications starting out as a Writer.

Here's something I had written somewhere before:

I wanted to write, but no one would hire me as a Writer.

Then they hired me as a Writer, but no one will hire me on staff.

Then they hired me on staff, but no one will let me produce.

Then they let me produce, now I don't have time to WRITE!

Keep it in mind. There is a lot of truth there.

Now some Writers have been hired directly as Story Editors as well, but the rules still apply. Being a Story Editor requires more experience than most people think. I asked Frank Lupo (Creator/Producer of series such as *The A-Team*, *Hunter*, *Riptide*, *Wiseguy*, etc.) what he expected from a Story Editor. He went down a list of things and, with each one, my heart sank. When he was done, I said "I thought that was a Producer!" He replied "Not on my shows." I have since found out he was right. What SHOULD determine when someone moves up is experience and performance.

Now let me say a few other things about "ego" promotions or "vanity credits." I have watched several people who have been promoted right up the list to Co-Exec Producer solely because the Exec Producer had a fancy for the person. Now aside from alienating everyone else on the staff (I will admit to being one of the alienated in one case), it is bad for the person being promoted. For one thing, they are thrown into an expectation that they can't support. The Exec may handle them with kid gloves, but the rest of the business won't. The rest of the industry expects results. And lack of experience means that person will never be able to satisfy anyone, even with the best of intentions.

Even worse, many of these people begin to BELIEVE they are deserving of the position. Which tends to make them arrogant and cocky. And when that particular job ends ... they are screwed. No one wants to work with them. I've seen this same pattern happen too many times.

Another thing I want to mention is the "negotiated credit." Let's say you get a staff job on a series and your Agent will contract you to, say, a two year deal with options. One of the requirements of the deal is that in the second year, you have to be promoted to Story Editor.

Usually, this demand is NOT an option, it is set in contractual stone. The idea is that the company might not want to promote you and pay you more money when it can just keep you at the level you're at while, because of your commitment, still getting more work from you. You would think this will protect the Writer and it should. But I've seen it backfire. On one of the shows I was on, we had hired a writing team on staff. They were very good as Writers, but in the entire year, didn't meet the qualifications of Story Editor. But their Agent held us to the promotion provision if we picked up their option to continue their employment. We felt they would get there eventually and wanted to keep them as Staff Writers, but contractually, we had no choice. We couldn't promote them and we couldn't just give them the credit. So we let them go.

These Writers lost a staff job because of a mandated contractual requirement. Yes, we continued to hire them as freelance, but they didn't make as much money as they could have. If the promotion had been an option to BE negotiated, that would have been different.

In this business, everyone knows how much vanity there is behind the credits. And, at the same time, this business is big on titles. It's a double edged sword and I wouldn't expect anyone here to turn down a promotion if it is given to you. I would just say this: Always keep your responsibilities one step above you and your arrogance five steps below.

VII. How Did You Get Started?

So, let's take a breather. This really counts as an anecdote, so if you want to skip it get and get back to the meat of things, go right ahead. You might, however, want to see where I picked up a lot of the things I'm telling you now and whether anything in my first break can help you now.

Earlier, I stated that I switched my college major to Theatre. I focused on acting, although I was able to work all areas of stage while I was at school. I was a light manager, house manager, I did set construction, and costuming. When I graduated, I worked for another six months at Marineland of Florida to make a little bit more money before heading to … Where? I knew that I loved stage acting, which meant that I should head to New York. But I didn't like the idea of living in such a compact urban environment. I mean, hey, I was just a kid who had spent most of his life on military bases and was now living in a town of 14,000 people.

So I decided that Los Angeles, while big, would be better for me because it was more spread out. It was more like suburbia, or at least pretended to be. I had a Dodge pick-up truck and $600. Another friend, Frank, was also heading out to Los Angeles, so we took off together. I was in my truck, he made the entire trip on the back of a motorcycle.

I'll spare you the details of the trip. But when we got closer to Los Angeles, Frank slipped away as he had a friend he was going to stay with. I headed onward to find my cousin's house. He and his wife had graciously agreed to let me stay with them until I got a job and my feet on the ground. Anyway, I passed the Hollywood city limit at 12:01 a.m. on June 1st, 1980. I had arrived.

Once there, I looked for work. Not as an Actor, but just to make some money. Again, I'll spare you the details, but my first job was working for an answering service taking messages. At the same time, I was looking for acting classes. I found one called Dvorak/Vaughn. Wayne Dvorak and Roger Vaughn ran the school. I audited a class, liked it, and started with them.

Wayne and Roger were great. I really enjoyed their classes. One of the things that Roger and Wayne had started doing (in fact, I think they were the first school to do this) was to bring in working casting directors to meet with us individually. Of course I grabbed on this opportunity. While talking to the casting directors, I was asking them what they wanted to see in an audition. They all said that they were tired of seeing the same material. At that time, mostly Neil Simon plays. They could mouth the words along with the actors. They all wanted to see original material.

Remembering that I used to write little sketches for grade school, I thought "Why don't I write some three minute scenes I can audition with?" So I did. My scenes started to become popular. After a while, I could go to a showcase and be surprised to see one of my scenes being performed! One night, in 1983, I was in a showcase doing one of my scenes. Several other scenes of mine were being done by other actors. Afterward, the casting director, Harriet Helberg of *Benson*, asked me if I had written all those scenes. I told her I had. She said I should consider writing. I immediately said no. I mean, that was a lot of typing, lots of pages, I couldn't possibly do that. She insisted that I give it some thought.

So that night, when I got home, I did think about it. I pulled out a script I had gotten hold of and looked at it. Hmmm … It's a bunch of three minute scenes, one after the other, in order, following a story arc.… hey, maybe I could at least give it a shot. So that night, I started to write a script. I decided to try a *Benson* script since I was familiar with the show and since Harriet worked for *Benson*.

It took me two days to write the script. Amazing you say? No. It wasn't a very good script. In fact, I would say it sucked. But … it was FUN! I couldn't believe how much I enjoyed creating the story, the characters, giving them dialogue, playing them off each other! I was hooked! I had to write another script. And that's where it started.

A while later, I was working as a host at a restaurant called Womphoppers. It was located at the entrance of the Universal Studios Tour. It was a wild place where we, the hosts and waiters, were hired to entertain the customers as much as possible. If they wanted us to dance on the table, dancing we did. On the table. There were a lot of crazy and creative people there. While there, I met a guy named Burt Pearl. Burt and I hit it off immediately and became best friends. Burt was also interested in doing some writing so we started collaborating.

Now it should be understood that a writing partnership is not just something you can do with anyone. There is an old belief that a writing team has to be closer than a marriage. I can tell you, it's true. There is a lot on the line, creativity, ego, pride and so on. And, somehow, those things have to mesh together. There aren't a lot of people who can do it. Burt and I did. I'm not going to pretend that it was always smooth, but it worked. And we enjoyed working together. I think, mostly, we learned to appreciate what each other brought to the table. I was good at finding plot twists and strange ideas. Burt was extremely good at mining characters and finding emotional turning points. I tried to learn from him. I would love to think he learned from me. Whatever, we started writing scripts together.

Riptide was a new series on NBC back in 1984. It was from the Stephen J. Cannell Studios. Stephen J. Cannell was responsible for such series as *The Rockford Files, Baa Baa Black Sheep, The Greatest American Hero, The A-Team* and later successes such as *Hunter, Wiseguy, 21 Jump Street,* and others. The series *Riptide* was about three army buddies who operated a detective agency out of boat, called the Riptide, located in King Harbor, California. The stars of the series were Joe Penny, Perry King and Thom Bray. Frank Lupo and Stephen J. Cannell created the series and it was produced by Babs Greyhosky, Tom Blomquist and Rick Dumm. I saw the pilot episode and thought it looked fun. Lots of sun, beaches, blue skies and wise cracking characters. Burt and I talked about writing a spec script for it. We had, at that point, written five spec scripts I believe.

So I made a phone call to the Cannell offices. Yes, I just picked up the phone and called. Many times you'll hear that can't just call the production company, but … well, I hadn't been told that yet, so I did it anyway. But I called with a purpose. It was my intent to ask if they had a Writer's Guide for the series. I managed to get an assistant and I struck up a conversation with her. I told her that I was a beginning Writer and I was interested in *Riptide.* I told her I saw the pilot and I really liked it. That launched a conversation that wasn't just about the series or about TV. For whatever reason, this woman and I had a nice chat. Which, by the way, is an important thing to remember; people will take the time to talk to you IF you are pleasant and engaging. Which, I guess, I was. Anyway, she eventually told me that they did not have a Writer's Guide, but that the producers, Babs Greyhosky and Tom Blomquist, were currently reading scripts to find new freelance Writers. She suggested that we send them two samples of our work, through an Agent. She also underlined that we should not send a spec *Riptide* script.

This person did not get my name, I didn't get hers. It was just a phone call, but one that wasn't just enjoyable, it was going to change my life.

Burt and I had an Agent....well, kind of. He was someone who would submit scripts for us, but not really try to get work for us. It's called a "hip pocket" contract. We called him and told him to send two of our scripts, a *Magnum P.I.* spec and a *Simon & Simon* spec to the *Riptide* offices. When that was done, we forgot about it and moved on.

A month later, the Agent called us and said that Tom Blomquist had called and wanted to meet with the two of us. Quite thrilled, we made an appointment. Then we tried to come up with script ideas, just in case they asked us for some. We honestly had no idea what this meeting was about. We had no experience and no one to ask. We had never had a professional meeting. So on the appointed day, Burt and I dressed in our best Sunday-Go-To-Church clothes, jumped in my Toyota Tercel, and headed off to the Cannell offices in their six-story building on Hollywood Boulevard.

When we arrived, we met Tom Blomquist. Tom was (and still is) a very affable, easy-going guy with a quick wit. It took only seconds to divine his sense of humor (bizarre) and he quickly put us at ease. He told us that he and Babs (Greyhosky) had read our scripts and liked them. They wanted to meet us. So we headed down to Babs' office. Now, with a name like "Babs," we pictured a fifty year old Barbie doll trying desperately to hold onto her youth. Not quite. Babs was about thirty and looked like Veronica Hamill from *Hill Street Blues*.

It's hard to explain the first minute with Babs. She had just finished dealing with a freelance Writer who had proven himself to be a real pain. So the first words I remember her saying to us after we were introduced was "I've been burned by Freelancers before, so watch it." She then invited us into her office (to this day, she says she doesn't remember that, but there were witnesses!). Once in the office, it was like we had known these two people for years. The fit was perfect. Babs and Tom were smart, quick witted, funny and definitely knew their stuff. And much more important than all this, they were down to earth friendly. We laughed and joked and chatted for what must have been an hour. Within all this, Burt and I pitched them five ideas for episodes. We discussed them all. Babs and Tom said that three of the ideas were interesting. They told us to think about them and call them back in a couple of weeks for another meeting.

Couple of weeks? No, no, we were too excited to wait that long. We started working on the ideas that night. Many following days were spent at the Beverly Garland Howard Johnsons, munching all-you-can-eat fried clams and furiously scribbling on yellow tablets as we tried to break these three stories. We managed to get an angle on two of the stories, but the third one just eluded us. During this, a question came to my mind. If these three detectives lived on a boat, where did the boat come from? I called Tom Blomquist and asked him. He said he had no idea, they hadn't explored that angle. Burt and I started working on a possible story involving the history of the boat. In one week, we were ready to meet with them again.

We returned and pitched the two ideas we had broken and the new one about the boat. They loved the boat one and wanted us to write an outline for it. We were walking on air as we left the office, wanting once again to prove ourselves to them. In one week, again, we had finished the outline and turned it in.

A few days later, they called and set up another meeting to discuss the outline. Discuss it? We discussed it, dissected it, rearranged it, changed the story, and formed it into a true *Riptide* story. It must have taken two or three hours. When the meeting broke up, Tom asked me who our Agent was so that they could have Business Affairs contact him. I said that I didn't want to appear naïve, but, I asked him, did that mean that we got the assignment? Tom looked at me incredulously and said "Guys, you got the assignment two weeks ago."

To show you how new we were to this, when Burt and I left the office, Burt asked me how much we were going to be paid for this script. I had only done day work as an Actor, so I said that I hoped it was at least five hundred dollars since we had to split it. I was only slightly off. The minimum rate for a one hour drama script at that time was over fifteen *thousand* dollars. Doh!

But we still had to write the script. After our revised outline had been approved, Burt and I dove into the actual teleplay. Once again, we were given two weeks to finish. Once again, we finished in one week. We turned it in on a Friday and waited....

But not for long. The following Monday, I got a message on my answering machine (I still have the tape of this message to this day). It was Tom Blomquist. He said that he had read the script and thought we had done a really great job. He didn't think anyone else had read it yet, but he had already given our names to the producers of *Hardcastle & McCormick* and *The A-Team* as they were looking for Writers. You can't imagine how thrilled I was! But the good news wasn't over yet.

On Wednesday, I was sleeping on the floor with my girlfriend (no, I didn't have the money for a proper bed) when the phone rang. It was Babs. I was still mostly asleep, but I do remember how the conversation went:

Babs: "Steve? This is Babs Greyhosky."

Me: "Oh ... hey!" (still asleep)

Babs: "I read your script and I think you guys did a really great job. Steve Cannell read it and he only had one note. So were thinking that you two might want to have an office down here and work with us full time."

Me: "Yeah ... that would be great ..."

Babs: "Are you still asleep?"

Me: "Uh ... yeah ..."

Babs: "When you figure out what I just said, call me back. Bye."

And she hung up. As soon as the phone was back on the cradle, my eyes shot open! My hand was still on the phone. Had I just dreamed that? Did it really happen? I asked my girlfriend if I had just been on the phone. She didn't know, she was asleep. It took me two hours before I finally got the nerve to call them back to see.

I got Tom on the phone. Yes, it was true. They wanted us to be Staff Writers on *Riptide*!!!! Tom said that we could give two-weeks notice wherever we were working and start after that. I had long since given up the job at the restaurant and was making $130 a month putting ads in shopping carts. I told Tom that I wasn't too worried about burning that bridge! Burt and I agreed to come in the following Monday.

And that's it. At the time, I didn't know how incredibly lucky we were. Cannell Studios was the premier independent studio at that time, with several hit shows on the air. Stephen J. Cannell was one of the most down to earth, congenial people you are likely to meet. The entire company was like that. And the opportunity to learn this business working for him was something that I could only have dreamed of. And, yet, it happened. With the debut of the *Riptide* episode entitled "The Curse of the Mary Aberdeen," Burt and I began our careers.

Oh, and remember I mentioned this all started with a conversation with that unknown assistant? For decades, I had wondered who it was that I had spoken to. I had no idea, as I said, I didn't get her name. I didn't even know who she worked with or what department she was in. It wasn't until just a few years ago that, with Babs Greyhosky's help, I finally figured out who it was. Her name is Kendel Fewell. And she ended up being MY assistant. Go figure that.

Now I want to point a few things out about this story. This is as close to an "overnight success" as I have ever heard in this business. I wrote that *Benson* script in 1983, I was on staff in 1984. That's only ONE YEAR (actually it was thirteen months, but let's not quibble). And it's one year from a standing start. Remember, I had no training as a Writer and didn't even consider it a viable career until Harriet put the idea in my head. What makes this so unique is that the steps that occurred were absolutely textbook. See a series; make a call; get a meeting; sell an idea; write the script; get the staff job. Textbook. It never happens that way, not in such a straight line. Well, it did once. Thank God.

About three years later, Burt and I split up our partnership, becoming single, individual Writers. It was an amicable breakup and he and I remained friends. We did go our separate ways and each of us has had our own success. Burt went on to work on several shows and become an Executive Producer of *Touched by an Angel* at the same time that I was working on *Xena*. We laughed about the fact that he ended up on Christian, I ended up on Pagan.

Unfortunately, Stephen J. Cannell is no longer with us. He passed away in 2010 and, I can tell you, the memorial service was an incredible reunion of amazing talent, all there to honor the man who created so many careers.

And Burt ... Burt passed away in 2006. I still miss him. Although we had long since moved on down our separate career paths, and we didn't keep in touch as much as we used to, we were still locked together forever. One of my last conversations with Burt was where we discussed writing a script together again, perhaps a screenplay. We were going to do it when we got the time. But time ran out.

This book is dedicated to him for good reason. Believe me, you really wish you could have met him.

Okay, moving on ...

VIII. DEALING WITH DIFFERENT PEOPLE

There is no way to get into this business without dealing with people. Hollywood has its own social dynamic and set of social skills which you have to learn to do anything. You have to learn to deal with people because you will meet a lot of them. Many of them will be good people, some of them will not. It's up to you to figure out who is who. And, more importantly, remembering who YOU are in the process.

What about finding a mentor?

Yeah, finding those mentors are hard. I do know of some screenwriting classes that pair you up with willing mentors. Usually, Mentors aren't people you can just find. They find you. Don't think about calling someone and asking if he will be your Mentor. Chances are, he will say no. If he wants to do that, he'll come looking. If you allow yourself open to learning from people, people will want to teach you. You just have to make sure they understand that you want to learn. It's pretty much that simple.

Of course, the thing you have to be careful of is the person who claims they want to help but, in fact, just want to take advantage of you. This is hard to determine. Keep some things in mind: Your Mentor should be someone who you truly want to learn from, not someone who tells you they know everything. Your Mentor isn't a wannabe, this person is already successful in the field you want to pursue. This person isn't going to charge you for the experience.

Your obligations to the Mentor is that you don't demand too much. You take it at her pace and with her guidance. You don't obsess about the speed of your learning and you don't feel entitled. If your Mentor says she is too busy to read your script right now, accept it and don't say another word about it. Let them feel good about helping you, not pressured because you seem to expect the help.

A producer wants to help me develop a pilot script from one of his ideas. I haven't sold anything yet. He tells me he can get this sold. Do I do it or not?

This gets into the bad side of the business. There are a lot of cons and scams here. Think about it; most people are so anxious to break in that they tend to leave their common sense outside. They are willing sheep, happy to believe anything as long as there is a hint of a chance of maybe making some possible headway. You have to keep your head screwed on straight. Remember that con-people tell you exactly what you want to hear, that's how the cons work. And they have a convenient answer for every question you ask. The easier someone makes this business sound, the more careful you should be. But as with the Mentor, how do you tell if it's a con and not someone who really wants to help out and give you a break?

You ask questions. Not just of him, but of yourself. You do research. Is this Producer someone with legitimate credits? And I mean legitimate credits as a Producer in the genre that he wants you to develop? Does this person have an open door with people who can say yes (in other words, is this a person on the A-List of the studios)? If the answer is yes to the above, then you might want to consider it. But, please, keep in mind that I mean verifiable credits. Don't just take his word for it. Check. You have every right to ask questions and do your research. And once being an Associate Producer on a TV series or movie doesn't cut. Those people might go on to be very successful A-List talent so keep a good relationship with them, but at the moment, they aren't there yet. This person needs to have current, verifiable credits.

Next, ask yourself WHY he asked you to do this. You are new, you have no credits in this area and wouldn't be regarded as a serious contender in the pilot biz at this stage. And be honest with this answer, assess what you think HE thinks you can bring to it. If it's your talent as a Writer, then that's fine. Just be brutally honest with yourself on this. Remember that right now, to the rest of the Industry, you are nothing. Why are you something to him? Ego doesn't want you to ask that question, but your common sense screams it.

At this point, I have to make something clear. A Producer cannot and should not ask someone to write a script for free. It's unethical and it takes advantage of the Writer. So I can only justify the advice I am giving you with two conditions: One is that you truly love the idea that this person has presented to you. You aren't doing it just because you want to break in, you are doing it because you'd do it anyway. The second condition has to do with the ownership of the script. If you are developing a concept and writing the script, what is your Producer putting into the effort? Without payment, you should *own* that script. If he says that he is going to sell it, make sure it's understood that he will be optioning the script from you in advance and that you will get writing credit on this project.

If he wants to write the script with you, then that's a different situation. In that case, you are just two Writers writing a spec script and sharing all the results of your efforts equally. But if you are doing the writing, you are the Writer. Him giving notes on your work does NOT qualify as co-writing a project. If he doesn't share the load of the writing (and, yes, that means typing as well) then he is NOT writing this project.

Assuming that you are the sole Writer and he is a Producer optioning a script that you wanted to write in the first place, make sure that as the Writer and creator (or, at the least, co-creator) of this project, you are attached to it, no matter how it sells. If he tells you that you can't be, then you are no more than a hired hand. And if you're going to be a hired hand, he will have to pay you to write his script at WGA rates.

And get all of it in writing.

You have every right to ask for these things; you have every right to demand them. Please don't fall to the temptation to trust someone on this. Don't accept halfway excuses or answers. Don't do a bit of work until this is all agreed upon and is in writing. And no matter what, do not succumb to threats. And by threats I mean something as simple as "here goes your big chance."

There are those who might say that, since you don't have a career yet anyway, what's the harm? None, really, if you act professionally and decline. But plenty if you agree to something you shouldn't have. You are now attached to that person in a legal manner. They represent you and, consequently, anything they say or do can be traced back to you. They might use your script to attract a bunch of investors into putting up money for a production, then the "Producer" skips town. Who are the investors going to come after? You. This isn't as extreme as you might think, it does happen. Not to mention that your Producer might bend some studio exec's noses out of joint. That's going to reflect on you as well. And if the "Producer" is a total jerk, well, you will be judged by the company you keep.

Assuming that everything checks out and it's all above board, ask yourself if it's something you really want to do. Will you be happy doing it? And don't be afraid to walk away from it if you aren't comfortable with it.

Agents—Care and Feeding

First of all, let me tell you *my* Agent story. Keep in mind I'm a TV guy. I have had many agents in my career. But I can only point to a small handful of items on my resumé (a rather large one, I might immodestly add) that came directly or indirectly from an Agent. Everything else came from my efforts, reputation or people I had worked with before.

My first Agent did nothing except allow me (and my partner at the time) to use his name and letterhead. That was all we needed. We made the phone calls and set up the meetings. He sent out the scripts when we told him to. When we got our first assignment (which led to a staff position), he negotiated the contract (standard contract) and took his ten percent. Did I feel he didn't deserve it? Hard to say because everything that did happen led to my getting started. Did he work for it? No. And how did we get him? Well, believe it or not, by going down a list of agents and calling.

Another Agent took me on, then promptly let me hang on the vine. This was coming off of two series as Producer, and the guy got me one meeting (with someone I already knew) in an entire year. And, by the way, this was with what would be considered a big agency. So, I left.

I had one Agent who was a real hustler. Had several good Showrunners to recommend me to, but wasn't that good at getting me out to new people. And, unfortunately, all his Showrunners were friends of mine, so everything came directly to me anyway. Later, we had some major disagreements over some under the table non-WGA work (he said do it, I said no) and I left.

Another Agent was a good guy, great friend, and was a moderate Agent with a well-known agency. Trouble was, his agency dealt mostly with sit-com, I was a one-hour Writer. But he did get me an Interactive Movie assignment (video game), which is something I had never done and wanted to try.

Another Agent turned out to be a greedy self-centered bastard (not all of them are, by the way). Needless to say, we aren't really on speaking terms these days.

The longest I was with an Agent was seven years. He was a great guy and I still regard him highly. The fact that I stayed with him that long is less a reflection of his power in the business and more of the fact that I liked him as a hard worker and a personal friend. I never doubted his devotion to me, but the business association inevitably ended. Why? The association, for whatever reason (and there can be many), wasn't producing results. I had to move on.

So, what have I learned? Well, despite having to do my own hustling to get work, and despite the bad experiences, Agents are necessary. Aside from the role we wish they would play (getting you those jobs), there are the roles that they can play that we take for granted. Which is hand-holding; getting information; playing the bad guy to Producers; getting material for you; making calls that you would rather not; helping you rationalize something when you need it; and the free lunch now and then.

Is all that really business oriented? Well … yes. It all has to do with relieving the stress in YOUR life so that you can write. If they don't do *any* of the above, then you should start looking for another one.

A word on the Agent Abuse question: Yeah, we all do it. We all know how many Agents died on the *Titanic* (answer: not enough). We love to hate them and we hate to love them. The treat us like dirt when we're the ones bringing in the money, etc., etc. But look at it from the Agent's perspective: They are in a *business.* The must make money or close their shop. They have more than one Writer on their list. Sure, you only care about you, but a good Agent has to care about all of you (collectively) while trying to balance the profit margin that keeps him in business.

If the Agent has an opportunity to submit Writer A or Writer B for a series, and he knows Writer B has a better shot, well, then the Agent is not the best friend of Writer A that week. And the Agent has to deal with the fact that you might find out about it and ... *"ring, ring ...* angry Writer A on line two, sir." Then consider that every bitch and whine that you may have is multiplied by his client list. In your mind, you are the One; that special Writer who's going to take this Agent to the next level. To the Agent, you are One of Many who thinks the same damn thing about himself that every other client thinks and wants special attention.

So how do you get that special attention? You move up. And, yes, it has to do with money. The more money you are bringing in, the more desirable product you are to be sold. I was asked recently at a seminar what was the best way to get an Agent. I responded "Have two hit shows on the air back to back. They won't stop calling you." Frustrating, but the truth. And when you get to that level where people are calling you for work ... then you can think about going without an Agent. But even those who can usually don't. Why? Because we've become used to the idea of an Agent for all the reasons that don't make sense.

How do I get an agent when I'm just starting out?

Short answer: I have no idea. It's one of the great mysteries and frustrations of the business.

There is no set way to do it. As I said, I called agents on a list. Others knew people who recommended their work to Agents. The key here, and remember this, is that you have to show the Agent that you have the potential to make money. And that means showing them you have credibility in the business.

Yes, of course, you might find that Agent who responds to the material and wants to take you on because they believe in your creative potential. In fact, I like to think that there are more of those than we want to admit. But Agents (like most people in this business) are looking for someone else to validate someone first. If you have a script that has won some contests, that helps. A recommendation from someone in the business helps as well. Something that says to the Agent "See, I'm not the only one who thinks I'm hot stuff!"

And, as always, get involved in projects and seminars. Another very very important thing is to net-work. If there are classes that offer face-to-face meetings with Agents, consider taking the class. It's not likely you'll sign that Agent, but you'll get an idea of what that person is like and his business in general. And there is always the chance that he might ask people to send him material for consideration. And do I have to remind you to send him a "thank you" note after the class?

Okay, this is not really a list of what makes an Agent good or bad. It's just a short guide for helping you find a good Agent.

First of all, for all the newbies out there, lose the awe!!! People who are new to the business tend to have an "awe" factor when they meet certain people. Mostly with people who can hire them, like Producers. But it extends to Agents because, even though we all know the truth of the matter, we think of ourselves as being hired by the Agent, not the other way around. An Agent "takes us on," implying that they have the power of decision here. And, for a newbie, they do. But you have to lose that feeling of inferiority around them. Because if you don't, you will forgive anything they say and never ask them the questions that you should.

I don't care if you are meeting the newest Agent in the company or the established 60 year pro, you have every right to ask any and all questions you desire. And you have every right to demand answers (in a friendly way). And, most importantly, you have the right to turn them down if you aren't comfortable.

What??? Turn down an Agent? But ... But ... Do you know how long it took me to get this one? I'll never find another!

Bull. Your work, your perseverance, your strategy got you there. It can do it again. And, if it didn't get you there, then they want you for the wrong reasons.

Okay, what questions do you ask?

Ask who they represent. They may want to be close mouthed about this, but you have every right to ask. I recommend you do this research before the meeting. In fact, you should choose your primary list of Agents to approach by finding out which agents represent the Writers who work in your desired area. And not just the superstar Writers, the grunt-work Staff Writers as well.

How many clients of your style/type do they have?

Do they represent any Producers or Showrunners who could hire you or read your work?

Do they have good relationships with the studios and networks?

Do they return your phone calls within 24 hours? I find this to be very important, but you have to make sure you don't abuse the privilege and call them every day with nothing to say except "do I have any work yet?"

Do they pay for copying or is that expected of you? This isn't as important these days as most of the scripts fly through the internet in PDF. Before the internet, TV scripts were usually done on the Agency's dime; screenplays were your responsibility. But I don't think I have had to print out a hard copy script for submission in the last decade or so.

Are there any fees associated with this relationship? If so, walk. By WGA rules, Agents cannot ask for any upfront fees. They make their money on commission *after* you have been paid. No matter how it's couched (office fees, postal fees, handling fees, etc.) it's unethical.

Are they WGA franchised? If they aren't, I suggest you move them down to the bottom of the list. It is extremely unlikely that they have the TV connections you need, no matter what they say.

Are you to be handled by one Agent, or by all Agents in the Agency? It used to be you had one main Agent and the others helped out. Currently the standard is for you to have a contact Agent who works one particular area. The other Agents divide up the town. The good thing (so they tell me) is that the agents all can establish more intimate contacts with the studios and no one is stepping on the other's territory. However, the problem, as I see it, is that I know that MY Agent has an intimate relationship with me. I feel confident that he can answer any question about ME that might come up. One of the other agents and the studio wouldn't be able to do that. They could only push my resumé across the desk and tell what they were told. And, besides, they'll be pushing the people they handle individually. I don't like this, but it is the current process.

Oh, I should also mention something that makes getting an Agent even harder. Instead of one Agent believing in you, they all have to agree to represent you before they take you on. That means that meeting one Agent who loves your work doesn't mean you have an Agent. She has to convince the entire company you are worth the effort.

Why are they interested in YOU? They had better mention your work. Quiz them on it. Find out if they really read it.

What do they expect YOU to bring to the table besides your work? You have to work as hard as they do, maybe more, but they have to know you are willing to do what it takes. You are partners in this, you don't expect them to carry the entire load while you wait at home for a phone call.

What is their strategy? If you are a new Writer, acknowledge that getting you started will be difficult. They should have a plan. Again let them know that you are willing to do what you can to contribute.

How quickly do they read scripts? The best answer is overnight. But most will say they take a stack home on weekends. That's good enough.

Don't be afraid to ask those questions. If they get offended, then don't be afraid to pass. You'll be asking them tougher questions as a client. And don't accept half answers. People starting out are so anxious to get an Agent that they accept half- and non-answers. No, no, no. Anyone who gives half answers is hiding something.

So when you find out who their clients are, call one or two and ask them what they think of their agents. Then, if you can, find out who has LEFT them and call them. Believe it or not, you won't always get people who are unhappy. Many times clients leave for other reasons. Some may even say the agency was great for getting them started, but they went to another level and wanted that level of representation. Others will say that it just wasn't a good match. That happens.

Now, there are also some things that you have GOT to keep in mind with this search.

Keep in mind that Agents have a different perspective than you do. Art versus Business. They are more concerned with the latter and only concerned with the former as it facilitates the latter.

You are not the hottest Writer in Hollywood. Not yet. And even when you think you have become it ... you aren't. (important hint: you never will be).

Don't suddenly become someone new with your Agent. If he signed you on because he has faith in your one-hour dramatic writing, don't suddenly tell him you want to be a sit-com Writer. Agents feel safer when they can pigeon-hole your writing into a specific genre. It makes it easier to market you when you are starting out.

You are not the ONLY Writer in Hollywood. You are the only Writer who has your particular talent, but most people don't make that distinction.

Your Agent doesn't have to be your friend, but you do have to be friendly with each other.

Be professional at ALL times. Be professional at ALL times. Be professional at ALL times.

If they return your phone calls promptly, give them the same respect.

There are MANY agents in Hollywood and saying "no" to any of them is not going to ruin your career.

If you decide not to go with an Agency, try to call them and tell them before they call you. Or, at the least, write them a thank you letter and explain that you have decided to move on. Why? Because it's PROFESSIONAL.

And if you call them back for a follow-up and they don't return your call, don't worry about it. Don't take personal offense to it, just move on.

There are many people who go at it without an Agent. I would say most in that position probably started out with an Agent and got to a level where they didn't want or need one. Some, a select few, never had one. In Television, however, it is almost mandatory.

I recently gave a friend notes on his script. We are no longer talking to each other because of it. How can I avoid being the jerk he was when I gave him my input?

By understanding human psychology and taking a good honest look at yourself. Especially where "pride" is concerned.

When I do agree to read something for input purposes, I ask the person if they want the "Hey, this is great!" read or the detailed breakdown with the harsh truth. If it's the first response they want, then I can say it immediately and save me the read. If it's the detailed breakdown, they should be ready for it.

What Writers have to realize is that when someone reads their script, that person has become an "audience." They should look at it that way. No matter what level that person is, if they have a note or comment, it is an audience member speaking. You may not ultimately agree with it, but it isn't something you can really argue with. In fact "arguing" a read is ridiculous. Asking questions of the reader is not. There is a difference between saying "you just missed the point" and saying "did it come across in the script?" The first is telling the reader that her notes don't matter because she is just too stupid to see the obvious. The second, however, is a clarification of how well YOU got the information across. You can't improve a script with the first, only with the second.

In fact, when I give notes, I hate the phrase "you just missed the point" because my response is "then you should learn to write it so I don't."

I had a friend who wanted me to read a script of his. He had some money and wanted to write, direct and produce his own film. So he sent me the script. I was very busy at the time and had it on my list, but he called and said he was into pre-production and needed my notes by the next Monday. So I put everything I had aside and gave his script a read. It was not a very good script, to be honest. But as a friend, I took the entire weekend to make copious notes, I wrote in the margins, I wrote separate pages detailing my comments, I did more than I do on my scripts because he had a great basic idea, just a lousy execution. And, besides, he was ready to go into production. So I called him to give him my responses. Every note I gave him was countered with "you just don't get it," "you don't see it," "take my word for it, I know what I'm doing," and the like.

Finally, I stopped the session and I told him that it was obvious he didn't want input; he wanted praise. He wanted me to be amazed at his wonderful script and gush over it. He denied it, of course, but I said that I had given all my notes and that was that.

Now, I had started the entire session saying that my notes were based on my experience and my opinions. He could take and leave what he thought worked. So all he had to do was say "uh, huh." But he fell into the Writer's trap of confusing acknowledgement of the note with submission to someone else's creativity. In other words, he felt that by just nodding his head meant that he was agreeing with me and, therefore, tacitly admitting that he had done something incorrect. There are so many things wrong with that attitude. Aside from letting his ego get involved and becoming defensive, he didn't realize that an acknowledgement just means "I hear your note, I'm going to think about it."

As it was, he went ahead and made his movie. And I give him credit, he made it with legitimate money, paying all his actors under full SAG contracts and union affiliations. However … he later sent me a DVD of the movie. He has yet to ask me what I thought of it. My response would be that my notes and critiques still hold.

Taking notes is one of the BIGGEST art forms to learn in this business. I'll cover the business aspects of it in a minute. But, first, let's discuss the other side of the coin.

How do I give notes?

The other side to understanding this "art" is learning how to *give* notes. Giving notes to someone is not an opportunity to trash someone's work. It is, no more or less, you giving your reactions to the material and helpful solutions to problems. And the person you are giving notes to is not required to do them, so don't get your feathers ruffled when they don't.

When I read material, I make notes in the margins and on the front page. These notes are, initially, not to give to the Writer. These are notes for me to examine later on. The first time I read a script, I'm reading it to enjoy it, *not* to critique it. Still, I can't help but have internal comments during the read, so I make little notes to remind me where things stood out. When things occur to me that are part of arcs, story or character qualities (things that aren't on one particular page), I put a note on the front page. Then, I go back and reread the script, paying more attention to my little notes than the actual story. I'm looking to see if, in total context, whether my notes and questions have any validity. If I have any suggestions or ideas, I'll note them in the margins as "what if?" When I'm done reading, I'll sit and think about what I just read and write my overall impressions on the front page.

Next, when I finally talk to the Writer, I ask questions first. This is to make sure that I didn't miss something. These are questions that I wrote on the front page after I was done reading. One of the basic questions I ask is "Pitch me your story as if I haven't heard anything about it." This is to give me the idea of what the Writer wanted to get across. It tells me whether he succeeded or not and where I can focus my input.

But many of the notes and questions you might have can be easily explained by the Writer as something you missed. Even though the "You missed the point" reply is often just defensiveness for bad writing, there is always the chance that you actually did miss something. If it was honestly your mistake and you realize it upon explanation, then acknowledge it and move on. If it was something that you missed because the script didn't bring it out properly, that's a note to be addressed.

Next, I give my overall impressions. These notes are also on the front page. What I thought of the story, the characters, the structure, and so on. These are general notes and, in most cases, the Writer will ask for examples. I respond that "I have examples of this when we get into the script."

Now I actually get into the script. This means I start at page one and move through it. I won't have notes on every page and that's fine. If it's a clean page, I just move on. I only address the things that I've made note of.

At this point, I have to make a distinction that is hard for Writers, professional and amateur, to understand: You are giving notes on someone's script; you are *not trying to rewrite their script*. Don't get into the habit of giving a note by telling them how you'd do it better. The temptation is there. Our creative juices get flowing and we want to use them. No, avoid it. You are there to point out problems (as you see them) and allow the Writer to find the solutions if she chooses to.

Scripts are as individual as the person who is writing them. They are very subjective. Many notes are "Taster's choice," meaning that one person would do it this way, another would do it that way, and so on. The Writer makes the final interpretation of the notes.

When you are done going through the script, you sum up your feelings about it. And try to be positive. Keep in mind that this person actually sat down and typed 120 pages of a story. That's a lot more than most people do.

And, for the person who is getting the notes, remember that your friend just spent an evening reading your script and making the effort to help you. No matter how much you hate the notes, he did you a huge favor and should be thanked for it. Appreciate the time and effort.

Speaking of time, when you set the time for you to get together to discuss notes, set a huge chunk of time. It hasn't been unusual for me to start at late breakfast for a notes discussion and work until we have coffee near closing time. And, by the way, if it's your script, understand it doesn't mean your script is a complete mess. It means you have something WORTH spending the time on. Otherwise the other person wouldn't waste his time.

What about getting notes in a business setting?

In many ways, this is very much the same. But there are important differences. Many of those differences have to do with politics and power. You have to pay a lot more attention to what the notes say in this case because you are being paid to provide the script that they want. The notes have much more weight and you are forced to give more than you would normally with a friend. In short, when you are just writing a spec script, you are writing it for your own satisfaction, so you are the final arbiter of the note's worth. In the business of Screenwriting, you are providing a product for someone else; you are the employee. You need to combine your sense of the creative with the needs of the entity that has hired you.

This can be an extremely trying thing for the soul. How dare these business people tell me how to tell my story, you think. I'm the creative one here! I'm the "Artist!"

Okay, let's dispense with that attitude right now. You are not an Artist. Which isn't to say you can't create Art. You are a Craftsperson whose work can, on occasion, be considered Artistic. Your primary purpose is to serve a business machine. Now, that business machine wants to sell a product as Art, but the *selling* of the product is the main concern. Cruel, cold, but true. It doesn't mean that your creative spirit gets squashed, but it does mean you have to keep things in perspective.

So what I am going to write here focuses primarily on this business situation. I want to talk about the room. I want to talk about the attitude. I want to tell you how every one of you can shoot yourselves in the foot in the most innocent of ways in an industry which is very unforgiving. I'm targeting the notes you will get when you sell your script or get an assignment. How you deal with getting your notes is a major factor in whether you get your next assignment. Especially in Television, but also in features. In fact, I get worried if I *don't* get notes. I'd like to think that my script was important enough to have an opinion on, good or bad. So you not only need to take notes, you should demand them.

First of all, understand that in this setting, notes are NOT meant to be an interactive procedure. It's a one way street. You TAKE notes in a notes session. The hardest thing for a Writer to accept is that this is NOT a discussion. Your baby is about to be dissected and you have to sit there and watch it.

You don't defend, you don't argue, you don't explain, you don't rationalize. Anything that you say that falls into those categories, no matter how well intentioned, comes across as resistance. And it makes the notes session into a discussion. It is NOT a discussion. Let it go.

But wait, you say, isn't this a collaboration? No, not really. But it also depends on who is giving the notes. And, perhaps just as important, what your opinion of that person is. If a note is given that you agree with and you see a solution immediately, you might suggest an alternative. But ONLY if the person you are dealing with is looking to hash out a solution. Most of the time they aren't and you might just get yourself in deeper water with a quick reaction solution. And if you are dealing with someone you have no respect for, then it doesn't matter what you say. So don't say it. Log it for future reference and let the notes continue.

As stated before, a notes session is NO PLACE for pride and ego. Now, you may end up with someone who wants to turn it into that. Fine, that's their problem. But you are there to get input, that's all there is to it. You aren't there to measure yourself against anyone else. Don't play their game; stay focused.

The first thing you should do when you get a note is to ask yourself what problem in your script led to that reaction. Don't automatically assume the other person is just an idiot and doesn't see the obvious. You may come to that conclusion, but it won't be an honest one until you examine your complicity in it first. Give them the benefit of the doubt. Explore the possibility that you, perfect Artist that you are, might just have made a mistake.

See the key here is to not get personally attached. Yes, I know, this is your baby, your sweet little creation, how can you not have a personal attachment to it? It ain't easy. Take it from bitter experience here. There is something I keep in mind when I write a script for pay. The first draft is my baby because no one has touched it. Past that, it's a product. I'll still have a pure copy of my baby to show off to friends, but now it's down to business. Stay detached.

Okay, but, even with the best of restraint, you are still human and you have feelings. There are pitfalls you could naturally fall into without realizing it. Emotional responses that might leak out accidentally. To prevent them you have to recognize them before they happen. What follows are a few of the most common ones.

Reactionary—Don't be amazed and appalled that someone has notes. Expect to hear some things that will outrage you. Or, at the least, make you feel the person you are dealing with is an utter idiot. Don't react to it. Don't get baited by it. Stone face.

Defensive—A notes session is NOT an attack. It is not a chance for someone to tell you that you aren't any good at what you do. It isn't meant to make you feel inferior and it isn't meant to imply that your script is substandard. There is NO point to taking offense unless the person takes a personal shot at you. And, even then, you had better be darn sure it had nothing to do with your script before you react.

Dismissive—Every comment and note is worth attention. I have gotten notes from a few people I considered to be, let's say, less than capable in the creative realm. But when they give me their notes, I take every one as seriously as if William Goldman gave me the note. Even idiots have observations and even if they are wrong, they can make you think. But ONLY if you allow them to. At the very least, if someone gives you a note that makes you think they just didn't get it, stop and ask yourself WHY they didn't get it. Was it your fault or theirs?

Argumentative—You'd think this would be obvious. But there is a very thin line between discussion and argument. The same thin line exists between explanation and argument. Same for rationalization and argument. Arguments have no place in a notes session. Don't start one, don't even start to start one. You won't win. You may make your point, but you've lost the session.

Explanitory—One of the things I don't want to hear when I give notes are explanations on why certain things were done a certain way. I don't need to hear it. I don't want to hear your inner workings or grand design. If it isn't there in front of me, I don't care. And it is very true, if you have to explain it, then you didn't do it right.

Here are the phrases you need to memorize for use during your notes session:

"Interesting."

"Good point."

"I'll have to look at that."

"I'm not sure I agree, but let me look at it again."

"Wow! Lots of stuff to think about! Thanks!"

And you have to say those things convincingly.

Now let me address what you are thinking right now. In effect, you are thinking "Well, doesn't this just make me the obedient puppy dog, rolling over and showing my belly? Am I just supposed to take all this and give the impression that I don't count?"

Not just that, but with that feeling, you have to bite your tongue and grit your teeth while you smile, too. And you know what the reaction from the other side is going to be? Respect. Not what you are feeling at all. The other person is going to respect you for being able to take notes objectively and professionally.

And if you don't take the notes professionally? Well, then it gets even worse. It's a human-interaction thing. Here's what I mean:

If you take the notes professionally and gracefully as I have described, you put the other person at ease. You give them the feeling that you are sincerely going to address their concerns. You may not be able to implement all of them, but they know you will give them a fair hearing. The result of that is that they leave the implementation and discretion in YOUR hands. They trust you to do what's right.

However, if you are resistant, in any fashion, they begin to doubt that you are taking their notes seriously. They see you as set in your ways and not about to make any changes at all. And when that happens, they become much more firmly set in the changes they expect you to make. They won't trust you to be fair, so they will start to DEMAND their changes get done. They won't leave it up to you. And when they get the script, they will go over it with a fine tooth comb making sure you did every little thing that they told you to do.

Getting notes that you are dead set against isn't something that happens all the time. But a lot of that depends on your mindset. And the rules of taking notes still apply. Even if you hear something outrageous, tell the person you will think about it. You don't want to be reactionary at that moment. Take it home. Think about it. Is there something in there you can love? Or something that you can do to address their underlying concerns and still get back to your original concept? If so, no problem. It just takes some creative thinking and that's what you are being paid for. If not, then the discussions begin.

I will tell you right up front, I follow these rules for the most part. I will also say that I have gotten into some pretty good knock-down-drag-outs with studio heads and Showrunners over notes. You pick and choose what you argue. But those fights came well after the initial notes sessions and were usually a result of greater problems than just one script.

I have also walked out of a notes session. Putting modesty aside, that requires a certain level of career where you can do that. And, even more importantly, I am prepared to keep walking, it isn't a bluff. Which is my next point. Never throw down the gauntlet over notes. Not unless you are ready to walk away. And keep in mind that you don't just walk away from one project, you walk away from all the projects that one was going to generate.

Now let's go back and talk about the "Artist" versus the machine. I'm going to touch on it only because it deals with the attitude people have when they get their notes.

Again let me make this clarification: "Screenwriters are not Artists. They are craft-persons whose work, on occasion, can be considered "artistic." If you consider yourself an "Artist," then go type up some "Art" and hang out at home. Don't sell it. Don't make a career of it. It's a hobby, not a business.

We certainly want to think of ourselves as "Artists" because that has a certain arrogant, self-controlled, individualistic feel to it. But face it, we aren't. We are businesspeople with a creative talent. We (Screenwriters) provide a product for a machine.

But doesn't that sound so cold? Only if you want it to.

You are only an "Artist" up until the moment that you sell your "Art." At that point, your "Art" becomes "Product" and you become contract labor. You are working for an employer and that employer is going to want what they bought to be fashioned in ways according to their taste and style. In short,

THEY ARE PAYING FOR IT. If you can't get your mind wrapped around that, then don't consider screenwriting as a viable career. Studios and Producers are not paying for arrogant attitudes and self-righteous indignation in the name of "Art." They are paying for a product. A script. And they expect it to be something they feel they can work with.

You: Employee.

Them: Employer.

A good Employer values the opinions of the person they hired. A good Employee knows who is paying for their talents and also knows that those talents have value to the Employer.

And, yes, even I hate putting it in those terms. But it isn't quite as depressing as it sounds. Someone is paying you for your talents and abilities. For the most part, they realize that it makes no sense to pay for something then destroy what it is that they paid for. So there are going to be disagreements, but obviously the Producer or the Studio value what you bring to the table. The notes you get are going to be a refinement of what they have already bought. In other words, if I buy a screenplay from you that deals with childhood friends who end up on the same baseball team, I'm not going to suddenly give notes that change the story into ex-marines who decide to form a rugby squad in order to fight crime (note to self: copyright that idea).

Now, does such a change happen? Oh, yeah. We hear about screenplays and teleplays that are changed substantially, so much so that the original Writers take their names off it. Here's the unfortunate thing: The studio can do that. Why? Because they paid for it. They bought it. Your artistic integrity is moot the moment you sell your product. You are in a business.

Now there is a tendency for some people to look at all this and start crying "Hack!" "Whore!" That's absolute B.S. and an insult to every Screenwriter who works or has worked in this business. I'll go back to the word that I use "Craftperson."

To put it into "artistic" terms, you have an idea for a painting. Someone wants to buy that idea. However, they have particular needs that have to be addressed. The room they want to hang the painting in is made up of predominantly brown and reds. So the colors you use have to be complimentary to that. And the wall that the person wants to hang the painting on only has a certain size space to fit into. And the person has a particular affectation for watercolors. Now that is no different from a development deal and getting notes. Your talent is that you are able to do something creative within those boundaries.

That is what taking notes is all about. If you are lucky and you play it correctly, the person giving your notes will make them general and allow you to be creative on your own. The other end of the spectrum would be the person who wants to stand over your shoulder and tell you which way the brush needs to move. Those people exist, but they aren't that common. And, as already stated, you run the risk of creating them if you are too resistant.

I'm sure someone will be tempted to bring up the names of Writers who defy the system and stand up for their "artistic integrity." First of all, the ones who are truly Writers (not Directors, not Producers, not Novelists, just Screenwriters) are extremely few. And for every one of those you can name, I can name several Writers you've never heard of because they sabotaged themselves getting notes. A couple of them are friends of mine. Some are people I've hired. Some are people I have been warned about. The commonality is that they don't work because they are too difficult to work *with*. If that comment came from one person, that's a personal disagreement. When it becomes a pattern, that's a difficult Writer.

Bottom line: Screenwriting as a career is a business. If you want to be in the business, you have to treat it like one. Which means recognizing your place in it. Your true talent may be in how you actually handle that interaction. If you can't deal with the above, again, consider another career. This one isn't for you.

So learn to take notes. I know mediocre Writers who have made careers on being able to do just that. It's that important.

What kind of notes can I expect while writing for a series?

Anything and everything. It depends on so many things. As a new Writer on the series, you probably won't hear 80% of the notes that the Studio or Network gives on your script. One of the jobs of the Showrunner or Producers is to get these notes and make the arguments before they get to you. By the time the notes do get to you, though, it means that they are a pretty much set in stone. Hopefully you'll have a good relationship with your boss, so you can either ask about the notes or you know which notes are up to you and which are mandatory. When I give notes to a Writer on my staff, I'll usually say if one is an ambiguous note (The phrase I use is "This is Taster's Choice") or I'll say that the note is something that they have to do, but I'll leave it up to them as to how they do it. Rarely will I tell them exactly what they have to do and how to do it. But that's me. Other Showrunners might handle it differently.

Let's put creative interpretation aside as far as this discussion is concerned and deal with notes that are production related. In other words, notes that have to be done because of production needs or limitations. As an example; you have written a wonderful scene in a train station as the two lovers realize they will never see each other again.

The mood is perfect, the crowded station behind them, the rush of the porters, the frenzied crowd all serve as counterbalance to the intimate moment between the two characters. Ah! Wonderful! "Sorry, babe, we can't get a train station. We've got an old gas station in the desert, we can shoot that on day five. Rewrite it." But … but…! This scene! The frenzied crowds…! The counterbalance…! No matter how much you argue, it doesn't change a fact: no train station. And the only place available is a gas station in the desert. Your job is to rewrite that scene without losing the emotion and intent of the original and still have it fit in the context of the story.

To me, the rewriting of a script requires more creativity than the initial writing of the script. You have gone from being a creative entity to being a creative problem solver. Personally, I love this part. You may hate it. Either way, it has to be done so learn to do it early. Embrace the note and look at it as an opportunity to create even more wonderful stuff. The train becomes a bus. The porters become an impatient bus driver. The frenzy of the crowd is replaced by the desert dust whipped up by the wind. And, in the process or rewriting, you discover new opportunities to elaborate on their dilemma.

More commonly, you will be told your script is too long. Cut a few pages from it. When you write your script, you are shooting for a standard page length that is unique to the series you are writing for. When the Producer reads it, he will make a mental note of how much time it will take to shoot it and how long the episode will be.

How do they do this? I have no idea. I actually don't know how it's done when I do it. It's a factor of experience; you just know. But the one person who will absolutely know is the Line Producer, the Producer who is most in charge of the mechanics of the production. It's his job to make sure things are done on time and within budget and to tell the Showrunner when they aren't. The experienced Line Producers have this strange mystical ability to just know how long a script is. I've seen this in action and I have yet to figure it out.

Anyway, back to cutting some pages. Most newbies tend to overwrite when they start out. Many established Writers still overwrite in their first drafts (I prefer to do this). When you go through it again, you'll see things that need to be tightened or can be reworded. For example, in dialogue, there is a tendency to write "prep" words or phrases. Such as:

CARL
Well, this is something we have to deal
with.

In that example, the word "Well" isn't really necessary. And, what you might not have noticed when you were writing it is how many times there is a prep word like "well." When I rewrite my script, I have a rule that any dialogue that begins with a word or phrase with a comma is immediately suspect. This includes "You know," and "So," and the like.

Another, which is a pet peeve of mine, is the tendency to constantly repeat the name of the person the character is talking to. Not just in one sentence, but in several sentences throughout a scene. This is really a matter of the Writer "hearing" the dialogue in her head, but not processing how it would sound out loud. One time in a scene is fine, but if you see it happening more than once, it is suspect. Delete it.

Why is this important? Because it is dialogue. It has to be said in a natural manner by an Actor. And those prep words and constant name referrals aren't natural dialogue. Prove it to yourself with a simple test. Read your script out loud. In fact, I do this all the time and I recommend you do it as a matter of course. Read your script out loud. Or have friends read your script out loud to you. As Writers, we tend to look at what we have written as something to be read. It isn't. At least it isn't intended to stay that way. It may make perfect sense on the page, but trip and fumble on the tongue. Better that you catch it before the Actor does. Your material starts to lose the trust of the Actors when you make it too difficult for them to interpret.

There are other notes from a production standpoint that will just make you laugh. Product placement is one that is popular these days. That means that the Studio or Network has made a deal with a company to feature their product within the series. So the line:

              CARL
Hand me that soda while you're over
             there.

Becomes;

              CARL
Hand me that can of Zippy Cola while
         you're over there.

If you do it carefully, product placement isn't that difficult to work with. Sometimes, it might not have anything to do with dialogue, but with, say, a sign in the back of a bar. As long as it's visible, even if it's in the background, it is still product placement. But when you do have to put it in dialogue, try to be creative without making it obvious that you are, basically, writing a commercial.

As they say; it's ShowBIZ, not ShowART.

IX. SOME CREATIVE ASPECTS OF YOUR SCRIPT

There are two schools of thought about Creativity. Some say you can teach it, some say it is a gift that you either have or don't have. Personally, I don't think you can teach creativity. You either have it or you don't. I do think, however, that you can be taught to release your creativity. The majority of the work is on your shoulders. You have to find it, you have to recognize it, you have to discover where and when it is best suited. And you have to do that without fooling yourself in the process. Not an easy task.

So, as to writing scripts, I'm just going to talk about some random elements that seem to be problems with a lot of people. I'm not going to pretend that I am able to teach creativity, but maybe I can show you a few tricks to use in the course of discovering your own.

How do you start?

I don't know. How do *you* start? This is an extremely personal and individual question. Everyone is different. The first thing I would say is that you have to have something to say. A script has a purpose. Whether it's a message that you want to get out or just to entertain, it has a purpose. Decide what that is.

Many times you will hear people say that you can't write a script without a "theme." That's probably true for most cases, but I think you can get so locked on figuring out the theme that you forget to tell an entertaining story. Honestly, I always get stuck when someone asks me the "theme" of my scripts when I'm writing them, but I can usually give an answer after I've written the script. Sometimes I just write and let the theme find me. We all have points of view and we all have opinions on things. Because it's a part of you, those things will find their ways into your script one way or another and will become a part of your theme.

I often get asked where my stories come from. I usually say "Everywhere." And it's true. No matter where I am or what I am doing, there is a part of my mind that is playing games. The games usually start with a little voice asking "What if ..." That "what if" starts to become an avalanche of curious questions that I have to explore.

For example, let's say that I am at the airport and I see a man buying a newspaper. Nothing unusual about that, it's a common sight. But a thought might pop into my head such as "What if ... that man is buying a newspaper for some other reason than reading it?" Okay, well that's strange. Why would a man buy a newspaper with the express purpose of not reading it? What other use would he have for it? To cover something? To hide his face behind? Or is there something about the paper itself that has use? And what use would require him turning to such a common thing such as a newspaper? What makes the newspaper special in its ordinariness? Well, let's see ... lots of security here and a newspaper wouldn't be noticed. Okay, that's something special about it. What about the paper itself? The ink smudges easily, which also means the ink can be removed easily and used. Perhaps to darken something else ... a disguise? And so on so on.

Does that lead to a story? Maybe. Maybe not. But it gives you an idea of how my mind works. I'm always spinning little fantasies from ordinary events. Most of the time, they are just ways to amuse myself. But other times they all come together in a story. I might have an idea about a great character and I don't have a place for her, so I file it in the back of my mind. I might read about something, a crime for example, that is interesting, but I don't have a current use for it. It gets filed. Then, one day, when I am playing my little mind game, all these elements might come together. Suddenly, I have a character, a crime and a unique situation and ... a story starts to grow.

Or I might watch something happen and spin a story from it, then throw in a twist. A man and a woman having a heated discussion. The man is holding a doughnut. The woman has her arms crossed front of her, obviously in a closed position. The man is gesturing with the doughnut, which allows me to create their characters. He has a point he's trying to get across, forgetting that he's holding a doughnut, and she's refusing to listen. I start to create what the argument is; is it about the doughnut? Is he apologizing for a personal slight? Has she rejected him? Or is he just an ass and she's had enough of his stories? Then, after I have a nice, tight story created between the two of them, I throw in a twist; I tell the story from the point of view of the doughnut.

Now, this is just me. Other people I know start out by saying "I want to write a romantic comedy" then try to find the situation that best suits that. Still others will read a story in the news that affects them and want to do a version of that story. Stories can come from everywhere. You have to be open minded enough to look for them. If you want a good guide on this, go no farther than the nearest child. They have what you want; an unbridled imagination that has yet to be restrained by "adulthood." Don't be afraid to play like a child.

Okay, I have a story in mind. What's next?

You have to decide what elements you want to incorporate into your story to best tell it. And you have to decide how to structure the story so that it flows in a natural manner. I'll say right now that there are many books out there that can tell you how to do that. I'm not going to go there right now except in very general terms. And this is *very* general as not everyone works the same way.

The natural flow of storytelling is simple: Beginning, middle and end. This is called the Three Act Structure and all stories have those same basic components. Your beginning sets up your characters and the situation. It shows the conflicts and hints at things to come. The middle shows these elements as they collide together, the friction creating more situations and conflict which will lead to some sort of confrontation. The end is how those different elements resolve. Sounds easy ... until you try to do it.

For me, I don't think about all that. I have this internal rhythm that I pay more attention to. I think most storytellers have that as well. The beginning, middle and end is a very natural structure. Many of the parts of your story will naturally fall into the acts that they belong in but you still have to consider where the other story elements fall as well. That takes some thinking.

To start with, you might have already thought about how you would introduce your main character or the situation. That would be at the beginning. Then, of course, you have figured out how the script is going to end. Good. You have your beginning and your end; you have found your framework. Everything else happens between those two points. Once again, it sounds so simple. Think of it this way: you need to tell a story. A story has a beginning, middle and end. So just sit down and tell your story. Tell it to yourself, tell it to your dog, tell it to your cat (as if the cat would take time to listen!). If you are a storyteller, you can tell the story. It might not be brilliant at first, but it's not intended to be. Just tell the major parts that you like in the order you think they would appear in the story. Then write it down, just the way you told it.

Okay, the basics are there, in front of you. What you're going to do next is make it into a full story, but not in outline or script format. You're going to write a Treatment.

A Treatment is, basically, a short story. It is your story written in prose form. It doesn't have to be long, although a Treatment for a 120 page script could be as long as 60 pages. It depends on your detail. This is mostly intended to focus your mind on the story and how the various elements play out in the manner that best tells the story. You want to be as complete as you can, but don't get so involved that you find yourself trying to write something that will appear in a novel.

This is just you writing out your initial story with more flesh to it, more color, more feeling.

By the way, many people don't even bother with Treatments. That doesn't mean that you shouldn't learn how to write them. For one thing, it's optional if you're writing a spec screenplay. But many companies require you to write one if they hire you to write a screenplay. And knowing how to write one will make you a better Writer.

I don't write Treatments, that is to say I don't write a readable Treatment. Mine are so filled with shortcuts and personal coding that no other human being could decipher them. But that's just me. I still write one that serves the same purpose. I have written them as full stories for production companies, but left to my own devices, I use my own devices.

Next, you have to outline your story so that you can write a script. An outline is called a "Beat Sheet." It will list every scene and a short paragraph explaining what occurs in that scene that moves the story forward. It will be written (for the most part) like this:

1. EXT. DINER—DAY—Find out Oscar is late. Hear more about the watch and why it's broken. See the bus with the advertisement. More comments about his ex-wife. He doesn't see the broken doorknob at first. Play that he hurts his hand.

2. INT. DINER—DAY—Oscar enters. Makes lot of noise. People stare. See waitress and establish

they know each other (maybe more than just friends at one time?) He loses the watch.

And so on. For a screenplay, this kind of outline might be twenty pages or more. It depends on the detail. It will be shorter than your Treatment and, as I've said, the writing of the Treatment makes the outlining much easier. For one thing, you've already worked out the order of things.

Once you have the Beat Sheet, you are ready to start writing your script. That is, filling in the details, action and dialogue that is the script's final form.

Okay, a few more things to remember. When you do start writing the final script form, you have *not* finished writing the beats of the script. In fact, you haven't even finished figuring out the story. As you write your script, you'll discover things you didn't think about, problems you didn't expect and opportunities that scream to be exploited. Don't fight it. Go with it. You might have a great idea that requires you going back to the beginning and starting again. You would normally want to fight that because it seems like so much work. But isn't it worth it to write the right script? Leave yourself open to the spontaneity and go with it.

Also, realize that you are not writing a perfect draft of the script. Too many beginning Writers make the mistake of thinking that their first draft has to be perfect. With that attitude, you'll never get anything done because you'll be constantly second guessing yourself. You'll go into creative vapor lock and freeze up. What you are writing is what I call the "zero draft." It's your first version of this script. When you finish it, you are going to go back and rewrite it. Then, when you rewrite it, you're going to go back and rewrite it again. And again. And again. And, then, you're going to hand it off to trusted friends to get objective input. And you will rewrite it again.

You might notice, at this point, that Writing truly does involve a lot of writing. I would say that a 120 page script might mean you will be typing 700 pages in total to get to the version you can send out to production companies and studios. If you think that is too much work ... don't bother with this career. Take my word for it.

Let's go back to the Treatment again for a moment. I want to talk about how I form my story. This is just to illustrate one of the ways that it can be done, but not the only way. Maybe not even the best way. But it's the best way for me.

I have my beginning and I have my end. I go to my work place (my office or my office here at my home) and for fifteen minutes I clear my mind of everything except the story. Everything. I can't repeat that more, everything. If my mind wanders for a second, I drag it back and start the clock again. All I want to do for the next fifteen minutes is just think about the story. It should be noted that I am not trying to structure anything or solve any problems at this point, I am just letting my mind flow with the possibilities. Not trying to force anything.

Then, I sit at the keyboard and I start to put in the obvious beats of my story. But, as I do that, I also type *anything* that pops into my head. Most of my thoughts will still be on the story, but I mean type anything at all, even "The neighbor's dog is barking." With the way my mind works, I know that since I have spent so much time thinking solely of the story, almost anything that pops into my head is going to have a slant toward that story or my mind is going to try to connect it to the story. So, as I am typing in these thoughts, I begin to notice that certain things seem to match together. If I move this one here and that one there ... that looks like a scene happening. And these two things together could be where the villain is first recognized. And over here....

See, what I've done is not just focused my mind on the story, I've made anything and everything around me something that is colored by the perspective of my story. Even the neighbor's barking dog might end up being "The neighbor's dog barks at Tony, which is how we know he was in the house." After a while, I have enough there to break out of it and start to actually structure it in a Treatment form. From there, I can concentrate on my basic steps, my beat-sheet outline and put it into order.

Okay, so now you've begun to write the script. And you've opened a whole new set of problems.

I just don't know how to start a scene!

Lots of people fumble with this one. It seems simple enough, but it's tricky.

Start it "hot." No matter what the scene is about, don't start it at the beginning unless the beginning is absolutely crucial to the story. To use an extreme example, let's say you have a scene between two lawyers in an office. They are going to meet for the first time and get into a heated argument about one of the clients. In real life (remember that?) you might have one lawyer come in and say "Hello, I'm John Landers." The other says "Nice to meet you, John. Have a seat. Would you like a drink?" "No, thanks." And so on.

Now while this is legitimate dialogue, unless it says something about the story or characters, it's *boring*. You might think about starting the scene with a briefcase slamming onto a desk and one lawyer threatening to physically harm the other lawyer if he doesn't see some action. That starts the scene "hot," right into the active point of the scene. And when you leave the scene, get out early. Don't waste time with pleasantries unless it adds to the story and character development. In Television, you don't have time to waste.

I have a lot of character backstory to get out. Is it accepted to use flashbacks in film or TV?

The use of Flashbacks is not something you want to jump too quickly to. It can be a compelling way to tell part of the story, but too often it is the lazy Writer's way to get out of thinking too hard. In general, a flashback as a necessary part of actively and dynamically moving the story along is okay. A flashback to explain something just so we can move along is not. Understand the distinction.

Flashbacks are frequently considered good alternatives to exposition. This isn't quite true. Exposition is another necessary evil that you have to have at your disposal, but need to avoid.

In any script, the audience needs to know something about the character's background. Just as in regular human interaction, we pick up on small things that give us clues as to what a person is really like. If we've just met the person, they might be introducing themselves by telling you a bit about them. This is the easiest form of exposition because it is straightforward: I want to know about your background and you are going to tell me directly. That works in the real world. Not so well in film and TV. We don't have the time to hear someone's life story and most of the characters we see in a film aren't in situations where they could talk about it easily. If they did, it would sound forced.

In Television, it is even harder to resist using it and more important that you do resist it. Television is a "now" medium. It moves too quickly to get mired in flashbacks and exposition of character. However, what you have to do is IMPLY the character's backstory and stay consistent. Over time, the audience will begin to "know" the character and realize that she has certain traits for certain reasons, even if those reasons aren't specified at the time.

Let's say you have a character who hates anyone who drinks. He thinks that anyone who even drinks casually has a lack of strength and character. Okay, that attitude alone obviously implies a backstory. The audience notes it. But how to get it across? Instead of "I hate anyone who drinks," you go with this:

"I wish they would abolish alcohol."

"Don't tell me you never learned to drink."

"I didn't learn. Everyone learns. I was taught."

Okay, now that says that there is something even more interesting here. But you don't have to elaborate at that moment. You can move on. However, it will stick with the audience. It's just enough to say that there is more to this character than meets the eye. A few more oblique references like that and the audience begins to see a pattern emerge. This pattern tells them about the character without having to be specifically told.

When you do create a character, whether for film, an episode or an entire series, you should know more about that character than you will ever put on the screen. You need to be detailed, but only for yourself. Maybe 10 percent of it will actually be seen by the audience, but you have to know and develop all of it.

O O O

Anecdote Time: When I develop a series, I like to go crazy with my details. I remember a meeting I had with SONY publicity when I developed *Sheena*. I was there with all their department heads. They wanted to hear my take on things so they could formulate a marketing strategy. So one of them asked me "Tell us about your show." I started … and went on for almost two hours. When I was done, one of them looked at me and said "You are the most prepared Producer we have ever met!"

The reason I was so prepared was twofold. One: I love creating things, so I just have to sit at a keyboard and let the fun happen. I really have no control over it. Two: I had just finished producing five years of *Xena*. And I had been asked to speak at several conventions for the series. Believe me, there is not one executive in the industry who will ask you why there are no female centaurs. But when a fan asks you in front of thousands of other fans, and you know your answer is going to be posted all over the internet, you had darn well be sure your answer is convincing!

But even more important than knowing your character's backstory is knowing your character's disposition. I often tell people that I might not be able to explain my characters very well, but if you give me a situation, I can tell you how my character will react without hesitation. And that comes from being so familiar with the character that you intuitively know his/her attitudes toward anything.

Oh, and there are no female Centaurs because it's a sex-related recessive allele. The extra allele on the female chromosome cancels out the allele for Centaurism. The male chromosome, needs only one allele to make it the dominant. Theoretically, you could have a dual allele in the female chromosome, but that results in another genetic defect that is terminal in the womb.

I told you ... I have to know this stuff.

How do I get across my character's persona without having them talk about it in their Dialogue? Or Should they?

Get a book on non-verbal communication. Seriously, look for it in the psychology section of a store or library. As mentioned before in regards to exposition, it's better to imply something than talk about it. Scripts are not, and should not be, about dialogue. It's about what best tells the story convincingly.

One of my margin notations when I read scripts is "OTN" (On The Nose). OTN dialogue happens even with the pros, but it always comes off as amateur. It means that the Writer is taking the easy way out by having the character talk directly about things so the audience can easily understand. It may inform the audience, but it's not interesting or entertaining.

Many Writers still tend to do it for two reasons:

1. They haven't made the connection that they are writing a verbal AND visual script.

2. They have fallen victim to the incorrect belief that scripts shouldn't indicate any kind of action or just indicate minimal movement.

They ignore the use of non-verbal communication. Simply put, saying to someone "I am angry" is more "written" than seeing someone commit an act of anger. Saying "I am frustrated" is "written," breaking a pencil absent-mindedly isn't, but can convey the same feeling.

Non-verbal communication is something that we do all the time. Some research says that up to 90% of communication is done this way. It is the way we move, the way we reveal our body language, even the tone we use when we speak. It's the way we assess each other the first time we meet before we have even spoken. It's the conclusions we make by watching the way someone acts and reacts. You can do this from across the room. In fact, we do it all the time. It's called "people watching." In the extreme, it's called "Profiling."

Lack of non-verbal communication is the number one reason people get angry at each other in texts and online chats. Why do you think we created those hated "emoticons" in the first place? :)

Study non-verbal communication and learn to indicate it when needed. But be sparse when you do indicate it in the script. Repeat that, be SPARSE. Only do it when you absolutely have to indicate it in order to preserve the character's arc. Fully interpreting it is the Actor's job. And Actors love to work with this kind of material. You do it too much and Actors (rightfully) hate it. It's what I call "Marionetting" your Actor; treating him like a puppet. It's disrespectful and shows you have no trust for him.

How much can you do it? That takes some experience. You'll get there, but not before a few mistakes and heated conversations.

In general, though, here are some things to be avoided when writing dialogue.

The obvious—A man just witnesses his entire family killed in a train wreck; MAN: "I just lost my family! I hurt!"

Exposition—This is the telling of background information or backstory. It something that is unavoidable, but learn how to do it deftly. Imply, don't specify.

Working with stereotypes—No, it's not a dirty word. We deal with stereotypes all the time. You'll probably find a whole chapter on that in the non-verbal communication books. The moment you see someone, you begin to size them up and make your opinions. These initial conclusions are based on your predisposition toward certain things: clothes, attitude, stance, color, etc. Many of these are personal reactions, but you'll find most of them are conclusions created and reinforced by the social community. Which means that they are shared by most people.

Think about the word "profiling." It isn't just about race, it's a "look." Think about the old experiment of having a blonde woman in sexy clothes going into a business office, then take the same woman, dye her hair brunette, put her in a business suit and glasses and see how the same situation develops. (This experiment has been done everywhere from Universities to talk shows.) The reactions that woman gets are based on a form of "profiling," an assessment of her that is based mostly on non-verbal communication. Her look sends a stereotyped message to those watching.

Talking about the past—Relating a past event to someone is tolerable *only* if the person has no knowledge of the event. In other words, don't have one character tell the other character something that they both already know. "Remember when we tipped the boat over?" is okay. But don't follow it up with "Yeah, and you fell on that turtle!" "That's right, and my coat got hooked on the shell and you had to follow me in the boat a mile to save me." Booorrrriiiinnnngggg. And it's completely unnatural. In real life, we don't go on, telling someone something they already know, then bantering back and forth about it as we recreate it.

This is a prime case of the characters servicing the Writer. The Writer is being On The Nose in order to get out backstory. People don't talk that way. So how do you do it? Again, with a deft hand. No more than three sentences on the subject and IMPLY as much as you can. Or, if not that, then have the characters dispute the facts. At least the argument will be present tense and the information just becomes fuel for it.

Avoiding the cheat—Trying to express things without using up dialogue space is hard to do. But the moment you feel relief because you found a way past it … stop and reconsider what you are doing. Most Writers just want to get to the end of the script and are looking for shortcuts to do it. Even good Writers fall prey to this. But shortcuts still come across as shortcuts.

Can you write an exposition scene without dialogue—Yep. Happens all the time. And, usually, the Actor or Director will get the credit because it's so subtle. And, many times they deserve credit because they interpreted it correctly. But it has to be on the page to begin with. Most of Joe Audience thinks that Writers only write dialogue. Remember that scene when Indiana Jones was running from the huge boulder after he stole the idol? Just as it was about to crush him, he leapt through a hole in the rocks and fell to the ground outside in the jungle surrounded by natives? That was written in the script. No dialogue. Was that exposition? Well, yes. There was a lot to learn about Indiana Jones in those opening scenes because it told a lot by how he reacted to things, not what he said. Although running from a boulder that's about to crush you is probably a bit less exposition and more common sense.

Can you use "On the Nose" dialogue...? Sometimes—When is it appropriate? Well, consider when you have felt it was appropriate in your own life. People generally don't talk about what they feel. They are too insecure to do that, so they try to use verbal manipulation to guide someone to what they feel. That relieves them the responsibility and vulnerability of confiding in someone (more true for men than woman, but still true in general). But when we violate that rule, well, it stands out. The father who has been a stern, emotionless disciplinarian all his life suddenly saying "I love you" to his son makes a heck of an impression. Do it only when that impact is desired as a course of the story.

I have said many times "Scripts are not only about words." People don't go to a movie theatre to read words. They go to SEE a movie. And, if everyone has done their job, they FEEL is as well.

What is writer's block and how do I avoid it? Or get past it?

This can happen for many different reasons. In the story phase, you just can't come up with something that compels you in this story. You don't know what the next step is and you are lost on how to accomplish the things that got you so excited about the script in the first place.

Sometimes it's because you wanted to write a story that was close to you, either something in your life experience or emotionally touching in your life. But when you started outlining it, you realized that it was difficult to relate that to others. You realize you might be too close to the subject and it's just not relatable to others.

Other times, it might be because the thing that really jazzed you about writing was a one-note premise. Much like loving a joke because of the punch line, but trying to turn the punch line into a full story.

If it's in the story stage, you're lucky. You're discovering that your cool idea isn't really a story after all. It will, hopefully, allow you to move on to another project or make you work harder as a Writer to envision it.

When in the script, it's many times just a matter of brain fatigue. You are working so intently on the script that, at a certain point, it all starts to run together like watercolors in the rain. You feel that you've lost the reason for the story and the focus you need to complete it. You start second guessing what you've done and where you planned to go. You're afraid to take the next step, even though that step hasn't changed from your outline. You have no idea what to do next and just can't break through. You start to lose faith in your abilities and your story.

There's a thing that I call the "40-page block." It's not uncommon and I've chatted with other professionals about it. It's that moment in the script where the story starts to wear you down. You have a great opening, you have a great ending you can't wait to get to. But there's a lull where your enthusiasm fades a bit. And, for some reason, it happens somewhere around page 40 (your mileage may vary). But when it happens to me, I just accept it as a natural part of writing and I move on.

When this happens, don't feel as if you're failing. Don't start questioning yourself or your abilities. This happens to almost everyone, including seasoned professionals. When people ask me how I deal with Writer's Block, I honestly say that I've never had that problem. But what I really mean is that I know what it really means and how to get through it.

But is there a way to avoid all this in the first place? Hard to say. Pace yourself. Don't wrap yourself so much into the script that you lose perspective. It's going to happen, get used to the idea. If you don't want to plow through it, don't be afraid to put the script down and walk away. That's the simplest thing. You might try to rewrite what you have or think that doing another outline will put you back on track. And you should try those things if they can lead you to something. But before you do … back away from the keyboard and do something else. Play with your kids, your dog, your petunias. Go for a drive. Go for a walk. Go for a beer. Put the script out of your mind and let your brain recharge itself. And don't go back to the script until you feel relaxed and anxious about tackling it again.

I do all the things I just mentioned. And, most of the time, instead of holding me back, it leads to a much better script. I just recently had a revelation about a script I had put down. I wasn't sure if I was telling the story in the way that I wanted to, so I put it down. Two days ago, I had this great idea. Now I'm anxious to get back into it. How long did it take me? I put the script down four months ago. The point isn't the time, the point is that it finally came to me because I cleared my head and allowed it to come.

Writer's Block is your Muse telling you to go play with something else for a while.

X. THE MECHANICS OF SCRIPTS AND THE TELEVISION BUSINESS

Just a few thoughts on the workings of Television as a business. Most people don't even think of it in terms of "Business." They assume that they create their "art" and it's produced. That's just one part of it. There are still non-writing things to know and things to be aware of. The more you know starting out, the better prepared you'll be when decisions about your career have to be made.

What's the difference between network, cable and syndication?

There is the specific answer and there is the general answer. Since we are all mortal and have a limited amount of time on this earth, I will keep it general.

First, you have to understand the structure of stations in your area. Again, I'll try to keep it general. You might have six broadcast stations in your area on various channels. These six have to keep programming on the air that you will be interested in. To do that, they need to buy programming and advertise it. It's very expensive to do. However, they could just franchise themselves to a larger operation that provides established programming at established times with advertising already built in. This would entity would be a Network, like CBS and ABC, and that station would be your local Network affiliate.

Look at it this way. You have a restaurant down the street that sells hamburgers. It's owned locally and the owners have to advertise their product to get the customers through the doors. Since it's a unique place, the hamburgers aren't that well known, so getting customers to sample it is a big deal and not easy to do. The owners want to establish customer loyalty by making them familiar with their hamburgers. Now, think of McDonalds. Boom, without me even telling you where the McDonalds is, you already have an image of their product. You already have an opinion and you already know their menu. Why? Because you have seen the advertising and you have tried the burgers. No matter where you go, you can trust every McDonalds to be just like the McDonalds next door to your house. For the owners (or manager) of the McDonalds, they know that the national advertising is handled by McDonalds, the hamburgers are transported by McDonalds, the people come to know McDonalds.

Stations are much like that. And when a station becomes a Network affiliate, it is franchised in much the same way. Your local NBC station can be counted on to show your favorite NBC shows. The advertising is handled by NBC and the programming is provided by NBC. The audience comes to trust the station as NBC.

The major Networks are ABC, NBC, FOX and CBS. They are the on-air entities that buy programming and franchise time from the individual stations. And by "on-air," I mean that they are available to anyone with an antennae on their roof. There's a caveat to that as you realize that those stations are also available through your local cable systems and/or satellite system. But they were originally, and still are, on-air Networks.

Now that was *very* general, but basically accurate for your purposes. There are also the baby-networks (and they hate to be called that) which are also on-air, but they are loose affiliations of local stations broadcasting common product. They work much the same way except that they don't franchise as much time as the other Networks.

In other words, each station has X amount of hours of time on air. If the stations are broadcasting 24 hours a day, that would mean that they have 168 hours of time to fill each week with programming. A certain amount of that time is dedicated to their affiliated Network for Network shows. What's left over is the station's time and they fill it with series that they buy themselves, local programming or infomercials.

For Cable, it's a bit different. The individual cable channels are also Networks, except that they don't have to franchise local stations. They have to pay for cable access in your area. So the SyFy channel is paying for the local access, but your cable provider isn't just "franchising" one network. It shows many different "networks."

True Syndication are series on those individual stations which are not franchised, or series that occupy the time left over when Network affiliated stations aren't showing Network content. A series that is a Syndication show doesn't have a Network backing it, so it has to be sold to the individual stations. The stations that have no Network affiliation can air that series whenever they feel it will do them best. Let's say 8 p.m. on Friday. But stations that are affiliated with Networks can't do that. CBS, for example, has programming at Friday, 8 p.m. So if the CBS station wants to show this new series, they have to air it where they have time not allocated to the franchised network. Many times that will mean 1 or 2 a.m.

Understand? Good. You can explain it all to me someday.

How does this affect you? For the purposes of the professional Writer, there are many differences.

For one thing, the pay scale is different between the three areas. The Big Four pay the higher wages.

For another thing, they buy product differently. TV shows in Syndication are developed by a production company, then sold to the individual stations. Network series are developed by production companies then taken to the Network for approval. If the Network buys it, the show doesn't have to sell the individual stations. It will be a part of the Network programming. One stop shopping. Cable stations are similar to the Networks in this regard.

Then you have the stations such as HBO, SHOWTIME, STARZ, and the like. Those are in a distinctive area as they have a different profit model to base their programming. By "profit model" I am referring to how those networks get the money they need for programming. In Network, Cable and Syndication networks, they generally get their money from advertising. Commercials that are interspersed throughout the episodes. Those have "Advertiser Driven" content. They pre-sell the commercial time in order to finance the TV series.

HBO, Showtime, Starz and the others like that are, for the most part, "Subscriber Driven" content. This means that the money comes from people who pay for access to their programming. You pay for HBO, you are directly funding the programming. On Advertising Driven content, you buy a product from a company that funds the programming.

Does this really affect you, as a Writer? Absolutely. It affects the way you tell a story, it affects the timing within your scripts (accommodating commercial space or not), it affects the pay scale you work for, and the budgeting for production.

You need to understand the differences because subscriber driven is the path we seem to be moving toward more and more as the internet becomes the major delivery for content. Netflix, Amazon and other online companies are now providing original content series.

As I said, all this is very general. And, as you have figured out, constantly changing. The career Writer needs to be a bit of a futurist to anticipate the dynamic changes on the horizon and take advantage of them.

The details of market saturation and FCC regulations are beyond the realm of our discussion here. What I have explained here is the equivalent of saying that turning on a light bulb helps you understand the thermonuclear reactions involved in making the sun burn. For your purposes, all you need to know right now is that turning on the switch makes your world brighter, but that you need to keep looking around the room for other ways to turn on the light.

What is the WGA and do I have to join?

The WGA is the Writer's Guild of America. There is a Western division and an Eastern division (although they don't have playoffs). A while back, it was called the Screenwriter's Guild. Any Writer should research a brief history of the Guild to understand where it comes from and why it was created. I can't repeat that enough, you should really research the history of the WGA. You need to understand why the WGA came into existence and the purpose it serves. A good place to start is the WGA website located at www.wga.org.

Guilds and Unions are hot political subjects in this country. As such, you have to understand my feelings. I am not necessarily a WGA flag waver for the sake of waving the flag, but I am a loyal member. I have, on many occasions, disagreed with WGA policy decisions. And I have problems with a lot of the things going on in the Guild. That doesn't make me exceptional, it makes me a run-of-the-mill member. I don't know a Writer member who doesn't have strong opinions on the Guild. If you want to see a real free-for-all fight, skip the hockey game and go right to a WGA meeting regarding possible strike issues.

Instead of focusing on my gripes, let's just deal with the Guild and what it means to you, the new Writer.

No, you don't have to join the Guild. You can still work as a Writer. But you can't work on series that have franchised with the Guild or studios that have Guild agreements. That pretty much covers 90 percent of television in this country. What's left? Local programming for individual stations; animation, foreign television, and non-union films. Even though you can still work, the pickings are pretty slim.

When I say that the Studios are "franchised" it

means that they have signed an agreement with the WGA to abide by certain rules and protocols. This is known as the MBA, or the Minimum Basic Agreement. It not only sets rules and conditions for work, it sets the minimum pay scales for services.

The Guild also sets the rates for residuals and serves as a watchdog to make sure payments are made. In areas of dispute, the Guild will act on your behalf to resolve issues with Studios and Networks.

This is not to say that the Guild is perfect. But, in my opinion, the Guild was created to protect Writers and is an absolute necessity for a career as a Professional Writer in film and television. More, it's not that you *have* to join the Guild to work, you should *want* to join the Guild.

And don't think that you can cheat once you are a member. There will be times when you will be asked to write something without a Guild contract. No matter what your financial situation, I advise you not to do it. No matter how many guarantees you are given as to secrecy. It's too risky. You are playing with your career. The Guild can terminate your membership and you will never work as a Writer for a Guild Franchised studio, Network or series.

How do I join the Guild?

When I joined the Guild, it was a matter of getting an assignment for a script and paying the fee. Of course that was back when *The Flintstones* was a reality series. These days, the WGA uses a "units" (or "points") system. This requires you to accumulate a certain number of units within a set amount of time, then pay the fee and join. Selling a story idea is worth a certain number of points, working week-to-week is worth another amount of points, and so on. Selling a screenplay of ninety minutes or more will satisfy the unit requirements in one effort.

The two tiers of active membership are Associate Membership (still accruing your points) and Current (full membership).

Once you have fulfilled your requirements, however, you must join the Guild. And love it or hate it, I recommend it.

Obviously, for more info and to get up-to-date qualifications, visit the WGA website.

O O O

Anecdote Time: A while back, I was in a dilemma. I had just gone through a divorce that had cost me financially. I hadn't had a script assignment or seen any residuals for eleven months. I was looking at my bank statement realizing that I didn't have long to decide whether to sell my house or not. I only had enough money to last me a few weeks. Fortunately, I knew I had some residuals due from a series I had written a few years before. Those residuals would get me through another four months of bills. I needed an assignment.

I got a call from a film Producer, Tim, who I had been recommended to. He had a movie and a script but needed someone to rewrite the script. The lead Actor and Director had already been attached. Both were recognizable names. However, the Producer told me, they were not WGA franchised. I told him that by Guild rules, I wasn't allowed to do a rewrite on the script. He said that it was just production stuff mostly. Now there is a provision in the WGA that allows limited production changes on a script by a Producer. So I thought there might be a chance to do minor editing with a Producer's title, make some money and still be okay with the Guild. I told Tim I would meet with him and the Director.

When I arrived at the studio office, I was taken to a room and introduced to another Producer, Bob. The Director, Eddie, was there. They had sent me the script so I had already read it. It was a mess, very badly written. Still, I wasn't there to address that, I was there to talk about minor editing. The Director, Eddie, and I really hit it off. We started talking about the concept and the script. Slowly the talk went from a discussion of mere production problems to major story reworking and character adjustment. We spent almost an hour discussing the first two scenes! The Producer, Bob, wanted to talk to me alone, so we went to his office. This is my memory's transcript of the conversation I had with him.

O   O   O

BOB: "So, how quickly can you rewrite this thing?"

STEVE: "I'm a very fast writer, but I have a problem. This is a major rewrite, I can't touch it."

BOB: "Come on. It's not that much work."

STEVE: "Yes, it is. Major. And as long as you're non-Guild, I'm not allowed to touch it."

BOB: "First of all, I think you're wrong. And secondly, who's going to know? You want the money under the table, that's how it will be. Your name won't appear anywhere."

STEVE: "Can I ask you a question? Your film is SAG and DGA, but not WGA. Why?"

BOB: "We have five films going on here, if we paid you WGA rates all the Writers would expect it."

STEVE: "Well, I can't help you."

BOB: "This is stupid. No one is going to know about it and I'm sure you need the money."

STEVE: "Sorry. But thanks for the meeting."

O   O   O

As I left, his parting shot was, "I'll be expecting your call when you change your mind."

Okay, I was trying my best to hold down my anger at all the arrogance. I went home. Later in the day, I got a phone call from the first Producer, Tim. Tim said he understood completely what I was saying and that he didn't like it either. But wasn't there some way that we could come to an arrangement? Eddie, the Director, really wanted me to be on board with the project. He reminded me again that no one would know, it would be under the table. I told him that I couldn't think of a way to do it, but I would call the Guild and find out if, perhaps, the company would only be required to pay basic health benefits. Maybe that way I could work but the company wouldn't have to franchise with the Guild.

So I called the Guild and got Rob on the phone. Without using the name of the production company, I asked him if it was possible to work for a non-Guild company if the company paid into the health fund. He said, definitively, no. But as we chatted, he seemed distracted, like he was doodling or something. I mentioned it to him and he apologized saying that he was involved in the Guild possibly throwing out a member because he violated the rules. I asked him what the guy had done. Rob told me that this guy had written a movie for a non-Guild franchised studio and had been promised that the money would be under the table. No one would know about it. Then the Studio took a full page ad out in the *Hollywood Reporter* and listed the Writer's name in the ad! The studio that did this? You guessed it. The very studio I was dealing with.

I called back Tim and told him … well, I told him no. In very colorful and anatomically correct terms.

Oh, did I lose my house? Well, here's a funny thing about the business. Remember I said that the residuals would give me four more months? It turns out the company that owed me the residuals decided to try and redefine the terms of the contract. That meant that the Guild had to intervene and demand an arbitration. These arbitrations can take months if not years. I went from a four month buffer to having to sell my house in a few weeks. Reluctantly, on a Monday, I called my old real estate agent and told her I had to sell my house quickly. She said she would be out at the end of the week to do the paperwork. Okay, sad, but it's just the way things are. That's what you can expect in this business. You never know when things will become darker.

Or brighter. The day after I called the real estate agent, I got a call from a man producing a series for A&E. He asked me if I would like to produce the series with him. YES!

Then the next day, Wednesday, I got a call from Columbia Studios. I had gone to CBS with them to sell a series and left a spec screenplay I wrote as a sample of my work. CBS wanted to option the screenplay and have me write a pilot script for a possible series. YES!

Then Thursday, I got a call from Columbia telling me that the series idea I had pitched to ABC had been accepted and they wanted me to write a pilot script on that idea. YES, YES, YES!!!!

On Friday, I was on the phone with my TV Agent when the real estate lady called to have me sign my house away. I told her I had changed my mind. I had gone from having two weeks savings to a six figure income in less than five days.

That's how this business is.

When do TV shows start hiring their staffs?

You know, in all my years in this, I have never come up with a satisfactory response to that question. There used to be well defined seasons when there were only the three major networks, called "staffing season." But with cable and mini-networks, the idea of "seasons" have become less set. Officially, there is no staffing season anymore.

However … I've found April thru June are the main months, but it also depends on which level you are talking about. (and, even saying that, I can guarantee you that other people would have different responses based on their experiences). Staffs are hired from the top down. The Executive Producer is first, then down the line to the Staff Writers. Executive Producers have to be brought in as early as possible. Many times, if it's a new series, they have to wait until the series has a "green light" for airing before they can start hiring.

However, there is no set time that someone CAN'T be hired. Staffs rotate in and out. There is usually what I call the ripple effect; a series staffs up, then discovers that some of the staff aren't quite up for the show. They are dismissed (or their contracts are allowed to expire) and replacements are needed. Or a show gets a late pickup and has to scurry to staff.

And of course there are mid-season replacements.

The truth is, good and fast Writers are hard to find. A series will grab a good Writer and give her multiple episodes, even if the show has fully committed its staff positions. Usually, you'll first write a freelance episode and, off that, you might be asked onto the staff. That's happened to me a few times.

I actually got my first job in September after doing a freelance assignment in August. Well after staffing season was supposed to be over. And I have hired people late in a season when people drop out.

Treat it as if it is always staffing season.

Is There a pecking order when hiring a staff on a TV show?

In general, yes, there is a pecking order. It depends on who is the ultimate series power.

Again, the Executive Producer is hired first, the Showrunner has to be in place and choose the people she wants to work with. After that, it can be in any order, although in general it is from the top down. The Co-Exec would be hired, then Supervising Producer, then on down to staff.

The reasons for this are varied, but a major part of it is that you have to create a cohesive team. You have to mix and match the ingredients that work best for the team. And you value the higher ranks more than the lower ranks, so you want them in place first.

Another very important reason to do that is negotiations. You don't know how much people are going to cost. So you use your money first on the higher ups, who are generally considered more important to the show. As you head down the list, you begin to get an idea of how much money you have left for Staff Writers (I'll have a small addendum to this in a moment).

Now, in rare cases, a Showrunner might start off with someone in mind that they want to "mentor" or a Staff Writer they really want to work with who is not of the Producer level. But, even then, the actual hiring is usually held off to see who else is on the staff because of the money issue.

And if there isn't that much money left, then they will probably hire that person as a "virtual staff" (my phrase for it). That means someone who is given multiple episodes for a season, usually more than three, and, even though they are not on staff and don't have to be there for all meetings, are invited to attend whatever they would like. Usually, beginning Writers take advantage of this to learn. Because of that, they are serving as a staff without being one. But, by the same token, they are not held contractually to the series. They can go out and write other series if they wish. It's a strange grey area that can be abused, so the WGA doesn't support it. But it works out to the advantage of the Writer, so I don't bitch about it too much.

Now, the addendum I was going to mention about Staff Writers. There is a type of pay schedule called a "guarantee." Basically it's a guaranteed staff salary. For the sake of argument (and not using actual WGA numbers) let's say it's $80,000 for a twenty week period. That means that you are guaranteed to be paid a minimum of $80K for those twenty weeks, no matter how many scripts you write. If each script is (again, hypothetical) $20,000, and you write two scripts (which is a value of $40,000), you will still get $80K. If you write four scripts, you have written $80K worth of scripts, so you zero out.

BUT if you write FIVE scripts, you are over your guarantee by $20K, so you will be paid the overage at the end of the contract. The advantage here is that the series can conceivably get a Staff Writer who costs exactly what would normally be paid for the scripts anyway. And the incentive is for the Writer to write more to make the extra money. If the Writer writes less than is expected, they know that it risks their employment, but they still get paid their full amount. So all the incentives for the Writer to do good, quick work are there. And all the benefits of having a Staff Writer are there for the series. Also, there is a WGA provision for first-time Staff Writers that gives the series a break and encourages the use of newbies. Truth is, I think new Writers have a better chance at employment than experienced Writers.

How do I get freelance work?

Chances are, your first job in Television Writing will be a Freelance assignment. As already discussed, Freelance work is work for hire. You are hired to write one episode. You aren't on staff.

Here are the basic steps for getting Freelance work:

Your Agent contacts the Series and talks you up. He sends a sample of your work.

They read your work and like it enough to meet with you.

You meet with the Producer.

You pitch some ideas.

The Producer likes one of the ideas and hires you to write a story outline.

You turn in the story outline, the Producer gives you notes and you rewrite it.

The Producer likes the story outline and you are told to write the First Draft.

The Producer reads the First Draft, gives you notes, they tells you to write the Second Draft (aka the Polish).

You turn that in. Your job is done.

For this, you are paid in three installments. The first payment upon completion of the Story Outline. The second upon completion of the First Draft. And the last, the Polish, when you turn in the final script.

If your contract is a Flat Deal, you will be paid the total amount no matter what. If they decide to cut you off at first draft and bring someone else in, you will still get your full amount.

If it is a Step Deal (aka an Option Deal), you can be cut off at any point without any further pay. Flat Deals sound better, but the Step Deal has a slightly higher payout because of the possibility of being cut off. The Step Deal is to protect the Series if it becomes apparent that the Writer just can't cut it.

Okay, now these basic steps to get Freelance work are, as with so many things in this business, the theoretical steps. If you are lucky, your Agent will book a meeting and you'll go in and … nothing. But at least you got a meeting. Or you might get a meeting, pitch your ideas, be told that they want you to write something and they'll be in touch and … nothing. Or you could go into a meeting and never pitch. It's going to be a different experience each time. The first thing you have to do is get the meeting. Half of that is on your Agent. The other half is that you have to have the material to get the Producer interested.

When is a good time to try to get freelance work?

When the show knows it's going to go into production. That's when your Agent should start trying to sell you to the Showrunner. You should also have your spec scripts in shape and ready to go. Start to do research to find out which new shows might make it to the screen and figure out which of your specs would be good samples for each. Strategize with your Agent.

But here's some bad news. Many series as of this writing are not hiring Freelance writers. Many, in fact I would say most, series are completely staff written. They don't want outsiders, they want to keep everything in-house. This makes it harder to break in for a newcomer.

The reason for this are creative and financial. Working with Freelancers takes more effort on the creative side as you are dealing with people who have to be brought up to speed on what you are doing and the very tone of the series. Staff writers live and breathe the series. This learning curve takes time and effort and, many times, still results in a staff member doing a rewrite of the Freelancer's script.

Most series will hire Freelancers if the staff just can't keep up with the demand. That was a true concern when you would get a pickup for a series late in the season and have little time get the necessary number of scripts ready for production. Many series, especially ones that are Subscriber Based, have longer lead times, so more time for a limited staff to write everything.

For me, personally, I always want to work with a nice balance of experienced staff and Freelancers. The reason is that I put a high value on new blood and fresh eyes. I think that the effort involved working with outsiders brings some outside vitality to the series. This industry thrives on new blood.

But that's me. And not every series I've worked on has followed my feelings of the subject.

What are the differences between TV writing and feature writing?

Well, my preference is TV. I'm not one of those Writers who hopes to break into film one day. Doesn't mean I won't write screenplays or jump at the opportunity, but my heart is still in the (ever expanding) small screen.

And I'm going to expand the question because the new paradigm of storytelling has its own situation. That paradigm being the long arc continuing series, such as *Game of Thrones* (or whatever is similar by the time you read this).

There are some very obvious script differences. The style of storytelling in TV has to be altered because of the need to incorporate commercials or, in non-commercial fare, continue threads in installments throughout the series. Also, TV series have continuing characters, so they have to be treated as such. The audience is more familiar with them but, at the same time, you have to make sure new audience members don't get lost trying to figure out backstory that the established audience already knows.

Films can follow the Three-Act Structure more closely. TV episodes follows a four or five act structure in commercial based series, and abandon the three act structure in non-commercial series while still giving the impression of a continuing story arc.

The pace of actually writing and producing Television is much faster than Film. You can take months to make a film. A TV episode has to be done in six to eight days. In film, you might shoot three pages of script a day. In TV, it can grow to ten or more.

In a long arc series, the entire season might be written as if it's an eight to twelve hour movie, then shot like a movie, but aired in one hour segments.

And, obviously, there are many more scripts involved to a TV series. Stephen J. Cannell used to say that every week, the script monster shows up and demands to be fed. He was referring to the fact that, during production, we go through a script a week (on average). The problem is that it takes a month or two to write each script. There is little leeway for mistakes. That monster has to be fed one way or another.

If you have what it takes to do Television (and it ain't as easy as you think), then you can make a much more consistent living than as a Writer for film. The funny thing is that many TV Writers profess a desire to break into film and the studios keep asking for feature Writers who will do television. Feature Writers, no matter how good or bad, have the taint of "quality" in the pretentious studio world. Very few of them can actually make the transition (and very few TV Writers can make the transition to film).

Finally, Writers get more respect in TV than they do in Film. That's just a fact. Film is a Director's medium; TV is a Writer's medium. In Film, the Writer writes one script and is generally out of the picture once filming begins. In TV, the Producers are generally Writers and the staff of Writers participate in the production.

Is writing for TV more satisfying than writing for the screen?

I happen to think so, but I love TV. Other friends enjoy working in Film. Start out by doing what is more satisfying to you. You'll still have to option of changing later. Not an easy option, but an option nonetheless.

What are the correct lengths for TV Scripts with Act breaks?

There is no set page length for TV series. Each show is different and each venue has its own time requirements. Network TV has a finished time of, say, 43 to 48 minutes (it continues to change), but syndicated timing is 43 minutes. Cable is different still. The best advice I can give for anyone thinking of writing a spec script of an existing series is to get an actual script for the show you are speccing (specking?

Spackling? Whatever, writing a spec script). Follow that as a guide … If the first act is approximately 12 pages, then you should emulate that. You really can't be thinking about the timing issue at this point. A 43 minute episode might well be 65 pages of script. Yes, yes, I know the old rule of thumb that says that each page equals one minute. Fine. We acknowledged the rule of thumb. Now put your thumb away, you won't be needing it (except for the space bar).

Commercial TV scripts are broken up along the commercial breaks. But one thing to learn is how to end an act. The idea of each act end is to give the audience something that will keep them there through the commercial. When you look at the script of the series (the real one, not yours) note how many pages it takes to get to those breaks and, more importantly, the "flow" of the script to that point. You have to figure out how to do it with your story. You don't want to outline an act and realize that it will take you twenty pages to write it. That's just too much time.

Ending the act is sometimes the hardest part. Not just finding out where to place the act break, but how to "pause" the story. I think in musical terms, but the end of the act has to have a final chord. Minor, major, inharmonic, something that gives a feeling to the audience. And that feeling has to have a question mark dangling at the end of it, a question that the audience can't wait to have answered and will guarantee they will return from the commercial in order to see.

Of course, we are now in the age of the DVR, so an audience member can "break" an episode at any time and speed up the episode past the commercials if it's pre-recorded. Nothing you can do about that and there's no point in second guessing what they are going to do. Just go with what you know and write toward the act (commercial) breaks.

Oh, another note related to writing the script and length. Scenes are generally no more than five pages at the most. Usually, three is the target. You can kind of figure out the expected page length of your script if you count the scenes in your outline and divide by three. Again, this is a rule of thumb. And again, the thumb is only for the space bar. Trial and error will give you a better idea.

I'm writing my script and I'm stalled. It's not writer's block, I just don't know how to make the next scene interesting.

Well … actually, it is Writer's Block. Or, rather, it falls under the heading of the previous chapter on Writer's Block.

But let's treat this a little differently. Let's say that this isn't a case of having your own spec script where you can take my advice to just walk away and come back to it later. Let's put some real-world pressure on you.

This isn't just a script, this is an assignment. This is for a current series and you have a deadline to turn in your script. You can't use excuses, no one cares about the dietary habits of your dog or his desire to consume mass quantities of scripted material. You are overwhelmed with the idea that you are stuck and you have a deadline. Missing that deadline isn't going to make you look very reliable. You're going to lose any chance you might have for a subsequent assignment and forget about the possibility of getting a staff job.

The script monster is at your door and he expects to be fed.

Just like regular Writer's Block, you just lose faith in what your outline tells you and you feel dry creatively. But you don't have the option of giving it a rest. When you are on assignment, you don't have the luxury of taking your time.

You already know the basic movement of your story, it's in your outline. So you know what comes next, you know what the next scene is for and what information has to come out. So let's say at page nineteen, you just stop and don't know what to do. The answer? Simple. Just type page twenty. That's all there is to it. Don't think too much about it, just type it. You know what is supposed to be there, but you are wondering whether it is good or witty or whether you're going to dead end … stop thinking! Just type. And don't intend to type well or creatively. Let your characters say just what you need to move on. Let the actions be obvious and clichéd. You just want to get past this scene. And if the next scene is the same … just type that, too.

As many writers will tell you, the answer is to "just write!" Write anything, no matter how bad you think it is. Don't try to think too much; just get to the end of the scene. You're going to go back later and rewrite anyway but, for now, just get through it.

What's going to happen is that you are going to have a finished script, finished in the sense that you have followed your story outline to completion. NOW you go back and reread it. First thing that you will notice is that it isn't as bad as you thought. The next thing is that you will want to rewrite certain things. In fact, you will get jazzed about rewriting. You'll do it. And you'll enjoy it. You'll love it. And you'll have written your script.

I actually have a similar problem, but in screenplays. I've done so many TV episodes that I don't blink when I write them (technically, I do, but you know what I mean). Film, however … my story structure isn't as solid or certain. So I get to my point, usually around page 60, where I say "what the heck am I doing here?" At that point, I go back and look at my story outline. If the answer isn't there … I just force myself to type.

How "perfect" should my script be as far as format and presentation? Doesn't a great story and characters make bad format and grammar irrelevant?

We're all in this because we firmly believe words have meaning. Bad grammar creates difficulty in understanding the words. Wrong words have meaning as well; the wrong meaning. And diverging too much from an accepted format makes a script difficult to read. If it's difficult to read because of misspellings, then, no, character and great story will not win out because no one will be able to see it through all the mess.

When I write a script, I go through it several times to make sure that it isn't a difficult read. Because I know what it's like to read a difficult script. When I started out and had my first staff job, I remember publishing my script and it went into general distribution. Soon after that Jo Swerling, Jr, the Supervising Producer, sent me his copy with red marks and spelling corrections. Now, at the time, I was a little annoyed. I felt the same way many people feel; "Hey, you didn't read the story! You were grading my paper!" No. As it turns out, Jo was telling me why he COULDN'T read my story. He had to spend so much time stopping his involvement to interpret typos and misinterpretations that he just couldn't give it the perspective it needed.

Every word has a meaning. Consider carefully what that meaning is. Every typo and glaring grammatical mistake has to mean something as well, and if it isn't what you want it to mean, then you have done the reader and YOUR SCRIPT a huge disservice.

So, you say, it shouldn't matter. After all, the audience isn't reading the script, they are watching the movie. The idea that typos, misspellings, obvious grammatical errors don't translate to the screen is extremely misleading.

Oh, yes, when the audience sees the movie, they can't see the typos. But the audience is not buying your script. You script is bought as a work that is written to be read, hopefully by someone who can then see your movie in their mind. But if it isn't there, in the words, the correct words, then you have started from a flawed beginning.

Honestly, I get tired of people who revere the word enough to want to make a career of it, then disregard the importance of the word because they just don't think it matters.

On the topic of spelling, I could make a list of words that make me stop my reads. You may think they are petty, but they still exist. "Loose" and "lose" have two different meanings. Learn the difference. Small thing? Maybe once or twice. But if a script is absolutely filled with those kinds of problems, I can't get involved in it. Most of these small things I try to recognize as being my own pet peeves, but you should still be aware that the smallest things to you can be bigger things to someone else.

And, you know, even if it is a small thing, this is a business where entire careers can be launched or denied by the smallest of degrees. So don't expect the reader to fill in the blanks where your script is concerned. This is a very unforgiving business, so it's ridiculous to try to break in under the premise that you will be forgiven for small mistakes. To a very small degree, individuals will forgive you. But, by the same token, individuals won't.

As to the idealistic concept that "talent will always show," I'm afraid people who say that always seem to miss the point. I am going to assume ALL of you have talent. I have to assume that because to argue it (for me) is pointless. You wouldn't know if you didn't have it and I don't have the knowledge to know if you CAN'T have it. So I make the assumption that everyone is incredibly talented and all of you have breakaway scripts. I take that as a given. So if we all have that talent, what's left to discuss? The BUSINESS. And having a script where words have MEANING, and, more importantly, where the Writer believed in those words enough to CRAFT them, that is seen as being professional.

Craft your script, don't just type it.

O O O

Anecdote Time: Before I broke in, I had a friend who was also interested in breaking into the TV writing business. This friend, Jerry, was already an established Writer, but in the area of journalism. He worked quite regularly as a news writer and magazine contributor. He had studied writing, had degrees in writing, and knew it inside and out. He decided he wanted to write a script. He picked the series *Magnum*

P.I. and wrote a spec script. He showed me the script. *Magnum* was a one-hour drama, which meant their scripts were about 65 pages long. Jerry's script came in just under 26 pages. I read it and, even though I wasn't a professional Writer yet, I asked him about the length of the script. His response was that he didn't think that mattered, the producers would see how good the story was.

First mistake: The producers don't just want to see a good story, they want to see how someone can write a good story within the format of their series; that includes the length of the episode.

Next, when I read it, it just didn't feel "real." The dialogue and the action descriptions bothered me and I couldn't figure out why, especially the dialogue. I told Jerry this and he agreed. But he said that it was perfect. It followed all the rules of grammar and syntax and ... a light bulb appeared above his head. More accurately, a light bulb crashed into his forehead. It was "perfect." It wasn't "real." Second mistake: Perfection is never perfect. We don't speak to each other in perfect Queen's English following the rules of grammar. We speak colloquially. It's a part of our distinctive character. Kudos for him for being the one to figure it out, but it was a lesson I took with me as I moved on.

You might think that I just contradicted my previous statements about making sure your script is a good as it can be. No, not quite. Dialogue is in a different category because it has to be spoken as naturally as possible. The grammar has to be colloquial, not precise. Grammar in your action descriptions are similar. Make it comfortable for the Reader.

Final note: Right now … I can tell … you are thinking about all the grammar mistakes I may or may not have made in this book. Don't bother sending me a red marked copy. I wrote this book as I speak, in my particular voice. Which is to say: badly.

How can I put my scripts out there when people might steal my ideas?

One of the most common questions and concerns of newcomers to the business. It's a good concern to have. It's also a debilitating one to obsess over.

First of all it should be acknowledged that Hollywood is not a pure and ethical industry. Most industries aren't. There are people who steal ideas. But the amount at which it happens is incredibly inflated. I would say that, in this era of internet, 99 percent of the accusations are made by people who were never ripped off in the first place.

I've been on both sides of this. I've had people pitch ideas to me that I've had to tell them I was already working on and I've come up with ideas that I've seen later on. Way back when *Remington Steele* was on the air, my ex-partner and I wrote an episode that had these elements: The clue was an envelope that smelled of fish; a strange man was stalking Remington; the IRS was wondering why the Remington Steele Agency paid taxes but Remington Steele never did. My partner and I sent it to the *Steele* offices. In short order, we got a call from one of the Producers asking us to come down to talk. When we got there, he pulled out the second season opener of Remington Steele. The clue was a fish. A strange woman was stalking Steele. She turned out to be an IRS agent. At this point, most people would scream "foul!" Since we had sent our script to them, they obviously had access. But, no, these episodes are not written overnight. This had been in the works for months. There was no way they could have known what we were writing and, in fact, they were writing this long before my partner and I came up with our idea.

Another time, my partner and I came up with a great idea about a detective agency that consisted of a washed up actress and a con man ... then *Moonlighting* hit the air. Same basic idea, but we had never pitched it to anyone.

But here's the big one. I wrote a pilot about a Chicago cop who chases a criminal down to South Florida and becomes involved with the local police there, a "fish out of water" story. If that sounds familiar, it's the plotline to the series *The Glades*. And, add to that, the creator of *The Glades*, Clifton Campbell, was a schoolmate of mine in college. Did he steal my idea? Did I steal his? A resounding "NO."

I was completely surprised when I saw his show hit the news and I know for a fact he never had access to my pilot and based his on different material (a play he had written, I believe).

Heck, just look at this book! Remember what I wrote in the Introduction about Max Adams and her book?

This stuff just happens. Usually nowhere near the degree of the incidents I've mentioned. But when we see it, most people want to think they are being ripped off.

There are many reasons why:

1. Some ideas just happen. We are all encouraged, motivated or inspired by events around us. We have to understand we are not the only people living those events and with the number of people in the industry, someone is bound to have come up with the same core idea at the same time you did. Multiply that by the millions added to the internet who have had ideas and voiced them online.

2. We all have selective perception. We look for commonalities and similarities with everything we do (it's connective reasoning and it's one of the basics of being a thinking being). So if we have (what we consider) a great idea for an episode for a series, we are more likely to look for things that are similar or parallel that idea, no matter how obscure.

3. The pride syndrome. We all have a sense of perverse pride when we think someone has ripped us off. It's like saying that we are just as good as they are,

so we tend to search for those things that show we have that equality and attribute them to ourselves.

4. We tend to ignore all the times they didn't do things that were similar to our ideas, which highlights those things that are.

5. We rarely stop and think about all the ideas that we see on TV that we had that the Producers never had the opportunity to rip off. In other words, the very proof that these ideas are rarely ripped off is ignored. If we have access to the people on a show (more on this in a moment) and see something that we mentioned to that person, we tend to think "Hey, they ripped me off." But if we have had NO access and see an idea that we came up with, we just say "Darn, I knew that was a good idea for them." The access determines whether we accuse or accept, even though the proof for either is exactly the same.

6. We overestimate the actual access we have to a show. I've dealt with fans all across the world on shows I've done. You would not believe how many times I have had people from another state or foreign country tell me that I used one of their ideas. Their idea of access? They posted it on a website and, as they know, I am on the internet. Whether it's that or that you told a friend who has a friend who has a cousin that knows a guy who makes iron fencing for Sandra Bullock, no, that's not "access." (And, for the record, I have no idea who does Sandra's fences.)

7. We ignore that fact that it is cheaper to buy a good idea than steal it. The repercussions are way too

expensive to take a chance on.

Recognize the old adage that you cannot protect an idea, you can only protect the execution of the idea. The more detailed you are with your idea, the more you can protect it. Just saying "In this episode, a gay couple moves in next door and we watch them react to it" is not even an idea by story standards. It's a notion.

Or, I have an idea about a murder mystery on Temptation Island with Hawaiian Tropic girls. (actually, it's a fantasy, but let's move on …). Can I protect that? Not really. It's too easy to rearrange. For example a murder mystery (generic plot point) in the Virgin Islands (not Temptation island, but same idea) with Victoria Secrets models (pretty much the same, but different enough). See what I mean? So what you are going to do is execute the idea into a full story and script. That is what you can protect.

No, you cannot be in this business and be afraid of being ripped off. But you also can't wade right in, naïve of the possibility. You protect yourself as best you can and move on. Which brings us to …

Should I copyright my scripts?

I'm going to go all technical on you for a moment and mention there is a difference between Copyrighting a script and Registering a script.

A script is copyrighted the moment you finish it. As noted before, this is not a notion or an idea, this is the actual execution of the idea. In this case, in a script format. Other executions of the idea would be as a novel or song. But for us, a script. And it is Copyrighted, by U.S. Law, the moment you complete it. No one needs to know that you have even written a script, it is a protection that applies the moment you have done it. As an aside, there's a whole Schrödinger's Cat essence to this. Your script may or may not exist as far as Copyright, but the Copyright still applies if you maintain it exists. But, just like the famous Cat, it's irrelevant until you have to prove what state it's in. Which is the point of Registration.

When you Register a script, you are time dating it through an outside agency that proves when you had possession of it. In other words, no matter how long you maintain that you've had your script, none of that matters until you can definitively prove when you had it. And you prove that by time stamping it in a legal manner.

You should, as a matter of course, Register your scripts.

There are several commercial companies that offer to time stamp your script, but there are only two you should concern yourself with. The Library of Congress, and the Writer's Guild or the Writer's Guild of America. Ideally, register with both. There are certain differences between the two, although both can be used as evidence in a court of law.

That's another important thing to know. Having a time stamp registration is not an automatic win in any dispute. It's one bit of evidence to be brought forward in your favor. Probably the strongest evidence, but not a slam dunk.

I'm a bit bemused when I see online forums arguing about which one to use and the merits of either. DO BOTH. They can both be done online and it doesn't cost much.

Oh, as a final note; when you do Register the script, don't put the WGA registration number on the cover. You'll hear a lot of controversy about whether or not to do that, but in general that's seen as amateurish and overprotective, as if you are telling the reader "I just know you're going to steal my idea so don't you dare!"

I registered my script, but do I have to register it again every time I make some changes to it?

Now given all the above, is it going to make a difference if, in your execution of the idea, you change a few things? Going back to the idea I just used as an example, if you decide it's more dramatic for the Tropic girls to stay on the island instead of being rescued, will that change it enough to protect it again? Probably not, since the elements are still in place leading up to that. Or, instead of a shipwreck, it's a plane crash? Again, not really. Both are just common delivery devices that don't really change the drama.

So the answer is that it usually isn't necessary. It depends on how much you change the basic core of the script and the elements that play it out. But if it's something that you worry about, the safest bet is just to protect it again. It doesn't cost that much.

XI. The Job Itself

I get a lot of questions about what it's like to actually work in the business, on a TV series. More specifically, people ask what it was like when I got my first job. I'll be honest, it's been so long since I started out that those impressions have long since faded. I do remember, though, that when my writing partner and I saw that we had parking spaces with our names on them, we left the car running in the driveway and stood in them for five minutes just staring at each other. To this day, every time I get a new parking space, I take a photo of it. But the actual working day to day has become a blur to me. You quickly learn that the job is a job. It's an extremely demanding profession that has its own logic. And the more successful you are, the more demanding it is. So let's discuss a few random elements of the job itself.

Spec scripts (Again)

I've already discussed what to expect when you go into a pitch session, but let's talk a bit more about spec scripts. As stated, spec scripts are your calling card. They are a necessary tool of the trade. Without them you will not get an assignment, not as a beginner anyway. You need to have at least five of them. And you need to keep writing them. Don't write five then stop. Keep going. The landscape of Television changes constantly and you have to keep up with it by writing scripts that reflect current shows and trends.

The kinds of scripts you write, well, that's got another set of problems. The first spec script you write will probably be of your favorite show. That's just human nature, you'll know more about that show and you secretly hope your script will get you work on it. As already noted, you shouldn't send a spec script to the series you wrote it for, so you can forget that. And by the time you are established enough to have a shot at your favorite show, chances are it will be off the air.

Pick the genre of the series you would enjoy working in. One hour dramatic, sit-com, comedy, detective drama, whatever. Take a look at the popular shows and the shows that are getting critical acclaim and start working on those. Watch the series, get copies of the scripts, start thinking about possible episodes. Pretty much the same thing you would do if you got a Freelance meeting.

Once you've decided which series to spec, get a copy of one of the scripts so you can follow their format. Actually getting the scripts aren't always easy, but if you have an Agent, he should be able to get you copies. If not, search the internet to see if anyone has a copy of one. If all that fails, use a standard format that you can find in general screenwriting books.

Some people recommend writing a spec pilot or using a spec feature. As mentioned previously, yes, those are fine. Just keep writing!

When I do get the assignment, should I turn the work in early and impress them or take longer to make sure it's done right?

Here's what you are going to hear:

"No one gets extra credit for turning in their homework early. We want it good, not early."

The truth is, we want it good AND early.

By WGA contract, you are allowed two weeks to outline your story, two weeks for first draft, two for polish. But that's really something you work out with the Producers. Those time allowances don't always apply when the Script Monster needs his feeding. Most Producers are very nervous with Freelancers, especially ones they have never worked with, because they aren't sure when they will get the script and, more importantly, they aren't sure how good it will be. Chances are, no matter how good, it's going to require some sort of an in-house polish or full rewrite. And the staff needs time to do that. So the earlier they get it, the better it is on their fragile nerves.

The best course of action is to ASK. If there is a deadline, you will be told what it is. And you MUST try and get it in before that deadline. Don't try to fool anyone by being optimistic, you will burn that bridge. And if you have another assignment that you have to do first, at least acknowledge it unless you are POSITIVE you can handle both at the same time.

The balance here is that you have to push your productivity without sacrificing your creativity. 15 pages a day is extreme, though possible, especially if you are the Exec Producer. Around six pages a day is considered quite respectful.

But the truth is, a TV series never has as much time as you need. So follow these rules:

As always, ask what the deadline is.

Be honest and upfront about your abilities.

Don't make excuses.

If you are going to be late, call as soon as you know and make sure the staff knows. Don't just ignore the deadline hoping no one will notice. We will. And it will piss us off, not just because we didn't get our script, but because of your unprofessional behavior.

If you do manage to write it fast and you know you have a couple of extra days, start your rewrites. If you have a chance, you might call one of the Producers or staffers and ask some questions about what you've done and get a jump on things.

Always ask what software program the company uses. It does affect the time element and it looks good that you ask. It shows that you are taking their time concerns seriously. This doesn't mean you have to use their software, but you will give them a heads-up on how they will have to convert it to their system when you hand it in. That saves time.

Always ask who your contact person is. If you have questions, you want to know who to call.

When you do turn in your first draft, make sure you give the assistant your availability for the notes meeting. Again, this shows you are serious about their time restraints. It also shows you have the responsible mindset of a Staff Writer (something that can never hurt).

O   O   O

Anecdote Time: A Freelancer was told we were under the gun in a major way. I told him that I needed the script as soon as he was comfortable with it. I told him that I would love to give him two weeks, and if he had to take it, he should. But I really really needed this script early. You would think that at the very least, he would have known that the most time he could have taken was the two weeks. I received his script on the nineteenth day, well past the deadline (I had received no phone call). I call his Agent and asked what was going on. I was given all sorts of excuses but the one that really rankled me was that he "had to jump on this other project real quick." That's not just bad form, that's unprofessional and unreliable. And it wasn't like that other project existed before I hired him. And, by the way, this was a seasoned "professional." He lost his next assignment as we didn't have time to waste with full production going on.

In another case, I hired another Freelancer and told him he had the full two weeks for his story and two weeks for his first draft. During the story phase, he would call with the most banal and detailed questions on things that I would have taken for granted. I was getting really worried about getting the first draft because he seemed to struggle through the story. He turned in his story outline on the fourteenth day, which was right at the end of the time limit. We had a meeting on the story and sent him off. Again, he began calling with the small, trivial questions and I really started obsessing. Did he really understand the story? The questions he asked made me doubt he had grasped the very fundamentals of the series. I was positive we had a full rewrite in front of us and he was going to give us no time to do it. I was worried. My Staff was worried.

On the 14th day, he turned in his script. And you know what? It was the best Freelancer script we got that season. And I don't mean just relatively good, it was great! It got a small polish and we shot it. The lesson for the Freelancer here? Keep in mind that we start to worry for small reasons, but don't let that stop you from asking.

Another Writer had a list of reasons for not turning in his script on the appointed time. A list of tragic excuses, things that were going on in his life. We gave this guy every chance to write this script. Then we get a call from the Showrunner of another series who was a friend of ours. She asked why we were having him do so many rewrites. What? Turns out that he had an assignment from HER show and was using US as an excuse for not meeting his deadlines there. I don't think I need to elaborate on the lesson. There are no secrets that aren't a phone call away from blowing up in your face. And this particular person was someone who I used to call a good Writer and a friend. I call him neither now and he has lost a lot of work as a result of that incident.

Another Writer was a gentleman who was always dependable. If we wanted it in one week, we would have it in one week. Two weeks, in two weeks. The quality was always up there and he was determined to meet his deadlines. In one incident, he was supposed to turn it in on a Friday. We get a call Friday morning. He asks if he can turn it in Monday. We tell him that there is no problem. He apologizes profusely. Then, in a conversational way, we ask if he has company from out of town or something. No, he tells us. He had a heart attack and is in the hospital. He has his laptop and has been trying to meet his deadline but, as he told us, the darn IV lines make it difficult to type. So are we sure Monday would be okay? Okay, the dedication is obvious, and I don't recommend anyone sacrificing their health for this business. But the fact that he called and asked for the extension is what I was impressed by. From the hospital, no less!

Bottom line: Be professional.

Doesn't turning it in early give the studio more time to screw with it?

One of the things about Television is that there is a time limit beyond which you absolutely stop worrying about the script. When the last day of filming is done, the script is gone. That also means that the people who are telling you how to rewrite it disappear. It's one thing to get notes from fellow Writers, but sometimes Freelancers get a little annoyed when they get notes that came from the Studio or Network Executives. If you think about it, the time between when you turn in your first draft and the time where the episode is shot is the precise amount of time the Executives will have to tell you what to do to "fix" it. If you could shorten that amount of time, wouldn't it be worth it to hold off?

Technically, yes. But it isn't always a good thing. The popular and trendy way to speak about Network and Studio execs is that they interfere with the project, they nitpick, they have no story sense, etc., etc., etc. And I have certainly run into people who fit that bill. But the ones who know what they are doing are also a good audience. They are an outside perspective.

And (keep this in mind) they are the BUYER. A good Net/Studio exec will trust you, but will also give notes and input where it is needed. They expect you to give their input serious consideration and make the correct choice for the project. Occasionally, they will demand a change. But they are your PARTNERS, so when you have a deadline, try to leave room for the execs to read the work. In fact, look forward to it.

I, personally, believe it's a good relationship. It's also a maddening, frustrating relationship. I grit my teeth when I get notes. Not because they are necessarily bad, but because I want to believe that no notes are needed, the script is PERFECT! I also want to believe that Sandra Bullock has a private library of my *Xena* episodes and Anna Kendrick is searching the web right now for my phone number. To my knowledge, neither is true.

Do a lot of writers end up writing on staff on a series that they don't like because it was their first job offer?

Perhaps some do, but I believe that Writers <u>can't</u> write shows they don't like. They have to find something about the show that they like or it will show through. And, even though they might have initial success, if they really hate it, they will lose that job because their scripts will suffer. Whenever I have an assignment to write, no matter how I feel about the series, I try to find something that I can love and get enthusiastic about. I have to or it would bleed right through to the reader and the audience.

Now, of course, there is the scenario mentioned here, which is that a Writer writes a great spec script and is hired on staff on a show they don't really like. Again, I think that will show up in very short order. But the larger problem is that we don't really choose which series is going to hire us first. And it's up to you to decide this isn't the show you want to write for and say "no." How likely is it that a beginning Writer is going to say "no" to any offer on a series? Not very. Most beginning Writers are extremely thrilled to get their first job and are still in the process of learning, so they will find their enthusiasm in that.

The usual problem is the Writer who is "pigeon-holed." I'll use myself as an example. I started out in network television, doing detective action shows. Since my resumé showed that fact, it was hard to get people of other genres to take me seriously. Now, I didn't hate the genre I was in, but I did notice the resistance. What I enjoyed writing most at that time was fantasy/action. So I wrote a screenplay that was in that vein. People reading that got the idea I could write fantasy.

Then I was hired to work on *Swamp Thing* and, suddenly, I was a fantasy/sci-fi Writer. A few more shows later and I'm working on *Xena* and, then, created the most recent TV version of *Sheena*. Okay, now I am known as a syndicated female-lead-action-fantasy Writer.

Then my Agent suggests that I write something else to show I have a more network friendly ability (back where I started, actually). So I write two spec pilots, right down the middle, network fare. The execs who have read them have reacted with "Wow, I didn't know he could write this good!" (quoted from two of them, it shows a disregard for credits and the elitism of some Network TV execs at the same time). Now I admit, I've been lucky. If you look at my resumé, you'll see a wide range of genres, but in this business, you are only as good as your last two projects.

And a lot of Writers I know have had long careers, but complain that they got pigeonholed by their first job. It isn't that they hated the first job, they just got burned out on it. They want to move into more challenging areas but the business won't let them. That's where the major amount of unhappiness happens in these cases.

Professional Writers should watch a wide range of series. No one should become a Writer because they want to write for a specific show. It is very rare that anyone ends up writing for the show that got them jazzed about writing. I have had many cases where I have gotten a meeting to pitch for a series I haven't seen and had to ask for copies of the episodes so that I could see what it was all about. And I've had that asked of me. It's normal. You don't have to know every specific detail of a series to write it. But you do have to know how to incorporate the specifics you are given.

It took me a long time to realize how to avoid being pigeonholed in a genre. I made a comment to a studio exec one time about me being known as the single-female lead-action Writer of the moment and he corrected me. He said that I was known as a character Writer. At first, I just took that as flattery but, later, I had to think about what it meant. What it means is that writing character is more important than writing action or genre. Because good characters transcend all genres.

Now whether the exec really meant it or was just fluffing me, I have no idea. But I do know that the thing that I always find to love in a series has to do with the characters, not with the settings. When it comes down to it, isn't that what we all love? Yes, we may enjoy the action and the special effects, but we come back for the characters. It's their lives we are interested in.

Wouldn't a true fan of a series be the best person to write it? Consequently shouldn't you try to write for the series that you love the most?

Let's define what we mean. There are people who like a series and enjoy it. In that case, yes, if you like a series, you should try to aim for it. On the other hand, there are people who love the series who are FANS. "Fan" is short for "Fanatic." The *Star Trek* fan stereotype is the extreme example. But let's just say a fan is someone who doesn't miss a single episode and knows the series inside and out. Are those people the best people to write the series? Most likely not. There are very definite reasons for this.

I have worked on many series where there have been active fan bases and many of them write what is called "fan-fiction." Some of it is good, it's very well written. But the vast majority of it has little to do with what the series is and more to do with what the fans want the series to become. Because they are fans, they have an investment in the show that becomes emotional. They want to "fix" the show and make it into what they think it should be.

I'll use the old series *X-Files* as an example. You would find many fans would have put Scully and Mulder in the sack with each other by the end of the first season, certainly by the end of the second. For many reasons, that would not have been practical and, in fact, would have been a disaster. Fans tend to feel an ownership of the series that they love. And they feel very possessive about it. They believe that they know where the series should go, when, in fact, the Showrunners already know where the show is going. They just need Writers to get them there. It's the horse behind the cart. So, in fact, their knowledge and devotion to the show doesn't give them an advantage, it gives them a predisposition.

However, there are a very very few fans who can rise above that and detach themselves from it. I know this because I was actually a major part of one becoming a Writer on her favorite series. After I had left *Xena*, Rob Tapert (the Executive Producer of *Xena*) called me and said that he wanted to do something different, he wanted to hire one of the fans to write an episode. There were many reasons for doing this, much of it was because we had a relationship with the fans and I think Rob wanted to pay them back for their devotion to the show. And no doubt the publicity angle was there. However, neither Rob nor anyone else on the staff thought that it was going to be easy, for exactly the reasons that I have outlined above.

Rob knew that I had more contact with the fans than anyone else, so he asked me who I would recommend. Without hesitation, I recommended a fan named Missy Good. Now Missy had been writing fan-fiction at first, then started writing novels with other characters. I had gotten to know her and I realized that she was a very responsible person who was able to compartmentalize her "fandom" from her writing. So I called her at her home in Miami. I asked her if she was sitting down. She said "Do I need to?" Yes. Yes, she did.

Did it work out? Yep. She ended up writing three *Xena* episodes and one of my *Sheena* episodes.

And I'll hire her again when I have the chance. But that was lightning in a bottle. It's extremely rare and the repercussions during production of making a mistake in hiring are so great that it's not worth taking a risk on. The only reason I did it was because Rob specifically asked for it. He was already prepared for the risk. Give Rob Tapert credit for making a huge leap in what others thought could have been a disaster.

I've heard that TV writer's hours are insane. A typical day when you're writing an episode is getting in at 9 A.M. and not leaving until 4 A.M.

It all depends on the show and your position. Seriously, there is no way to give a set general answer for this. From my experience, usually nine or ten until six or seven p.m. That could be a bit misleading because you don't just work in the office and, if you are shooting locally, you may be required on the set from time to time. The hours that the office is open doesn't equal the hours you will have to work to fulfill your duties. As you move up in the chain, the responsibilities are heavier so your work load (and hours) become greater. My last show had me in my office around eight a.m. (or as early as six if I had to stop by the set), working until midnight (on production work), going home to write until three a.m. then starting over again. Sounds impossible and when I look back on it, I can't believe I did it. I'm still recovering from it. Learn how to manage your time so that you don't fall into that kind of pattern.

Okay, so you're on staff and it's your week to write an episode. What kind of hours can you expect to work?

Okay, the misconception here is that you write your episodes on a weekly basis. That's not the case at all. Using general Network series, let's say there are 22 episodes to be written. For some series, it could be as low as eight, others higher. But for this discussion, let's go with 22. When the series starts, the staff discusses story ideas. The ideas are listed in a very general one-line sense, hopefully 22 or more of them, but at least ten. Then, the Writers are assigned episodes to write. Usually you'll be writing one of the ideas you came up with and the other ideas you had will be stored for later. However, you might have a particular strength in your writing that makes your boss want you to write someone else's idea. And there's no guarantee you'll be writing your other ideas later. You might be too busy to get to them, so another staff member might pick it up or it gets assigned to a Freelancer.

Say there are four Writers on staff (every level) so that's four scripts to begin. From that point on, it's a rollercoaster. When you are done with the script you are working on, when it is in a production draft level, it is put into the production mix and you start on another script. During that other script, you will have to do further rewrites on your first script for studio, network notes and production concerns. As you are doing that, you are also in meetings for the other scripts as well as your own and meetings dealing with Freelance Writers.

When you are finished with your second script, you move into another one while still doing notes on the first two and all the other things. So on and so on until the 22 episodes are finished. And you hope and pray that you can stay ahead of the curve. Once you actually start production, you want to be way ahead on scripts. Keep in mind that each script ideally may take a minimum of a month and a half to write but gets produced at the rate of one a week (the Script Monster).

If you're lucky, you'll get an early pick-up on the series and you can get a head start on the next season's scripts.

Since you will be told when your deadlines for each assignment are, the idea of working specific "hours" doesn't apply. If I need your script on Tuesday the twelfth, you will work whatever hours you need to accomplish that deadline and still be able to handle all the other things required of you. The number of hours depends a lot on your writing style and how good you are at organizing your time.

What if you're not writing an episode but doing some rewrites on freelance stuff. What kind of hours do you expect that week?

Same answer. It's not a weekly thing. I know some people who can focus in on a rewrite and do it in a couple of hours. Others have to do an outline and re-examine all the variables. It depends on you. I'm in the camp that does the notes at the same time that I hear them. Not physically on the page, but if I am getting notes from the studio, I am already figuring out the details in my head as they are telling me. The funny thing is that it means I am usually very silent during the discussion, which sometimes gets mistaken for disagreement. It's not, it's just that I am thinking. No one mistakes when I *do* disagree, though. So by the time I get to actually doing the rewrite, I can do it fairly quickly because the logic has already been figured out. I've just learned it saves me time that way.

What is the day in the life of a TV Writer like? Is there a writer's meeting every day or are they once a week?

Again, everyone has a different experience depending on the series and the situation. You're beginning to see the pattern of ambiguity in this business. I'm sure you are getting tired of me saying "it depends" and, believe me, I get tired of writing it. Every series is different and is handled differently. The tone is usually set by the person at the top, the Showrunner.

There aren't necessarily meetings every day, but there can be. If you are a Producer, there will be a meeting almost every day on something. Whether it's a phone meeting or in person, something will demand your attention. When you are in production, you get dailies every day, so you'll want to see those. "Dailies" refers to the footage that was shot the day before. It means every take and every camera angle. Some series have everyone get together to watch them and others distribute the dailies to each person to be viewed separately. It becomes part of your day to watch them and keep up with what's going on.

You will also get production reports. You need to understand them and review them every day. Those reports tell you what is going on as far as the shooting of the series is concerned. It also tells you which scenes have been shot. I'll usually go through my script and mark the scenes that have been shot on a daily basis. That way if an emergency arises, I'll know exactly what I have left with which to rewrite (and fix) the problem.

When you go into work, you have a list of things that you need to accomplish that day, most of them are self-motivated tasks. And as the day goes on, other things will pop up.

And, by the way, a big thing for everyone to remember is the self-motivation thing. As I have said, you will be given a project deadline. How responsibly you handle that determines how long you will be there. I can tell you that it doesn't matter if you are the greatest Writer in the universe, if you can't be professional and reliable, you are gone. There are many more "fairly good" Writers out there who will work their asses off and, in the end, be better for the series.

There are times when I've had Writers who had very strange writing habits. One Writer slept in his office every day. But he was always there when I needed him, always on top of things and always had his scripts ready. Obviously, he was taking care of business. But if he had been out partying all night, sleeping during the day, late for meetings, not quite there during them, and turning in scripts late....well, he'd have to go. No matter how great his scripts were.

Oh, and by the way ... depending on how much you get done during the week, your weekends are just the same, except without the meetings. When you get toward the end of the season and the Producer realizes that she doesn't have as many scripts as she needs, you're going to end up doing a lot more weekend marathons. Usually, you'll team up with another staffer to write a quick script. In some cases, everyone on the staff will pitch in and write a script together. This is called (and please, I hope no one takes offense at this) "gangbanging."

Learn discipline. The more structured you are in your life now, the more time you'll have to yourself when you are on a show. Important lesson.

When you are on staff, can you write for more than one company at a time in television?

By your staff contract, you can only write for the "entity" you are contracted to. Most of the times, it will be for a specific series. However, if you are contracted by WifflePoof Productions and WifflePoof has "Oyster Shucker" on CBS and "Weeble, P.I." on USA, you might be able to write for both of them assuming that the Exec Producers involved are okay with that. If it's one Exec on both shows, usually no problem. But it's not your right to determine that. It's something that the Exec may ask you to do because "Weeble, P.I." is in script trouble. But by the strictest interpretation of your contract, you will most likely be locked onto one series.

Obviously this doesn't apply to the Freelance Writer. The Freelancer tries to get as many assignments as he can handle. One series can't restrict him from working on others.

Are series required to hire freelance writers?

There are WGA guidelines about hiring a certain number of Freelancers or interviewing Freelancers. I've never had problems with this because I usually hire several Freelancers each season and I enjoy working with them. But let me elaborate on the WGA guidelines:

An Exec Producer must hire a certain number of Freelancers each season (Freelancers means Writers who have not yet written for the series and are not on staff and the number is determined on the number of episodes ordered).

OR

An Exec Producer (or the person who has the capability to green light a script) must hear pitches from a minimum number of Freelancers (that number determined by the number of episodes ordered).

The idea, obviously, is to provide access to other outside Writers and prevent staffs from eating up all the assignments. Now for those of you who think that a company could get around it just by doing the required interviews, it's not that easy. The important parts of the guideline are the number of pitches required (a lot) and the fact that a "yes" person has to be involved in the meeting. That means a person who can actually give the assignment to the Writer. Usually that's the Exec Producer.

I mentioned earlier that the bad news here is that less series are hiring Freelancers than they used to. Obviously the intent of this rule has now been long forgotten, to the detriment of storytelling, in my opinion.

I was told a first time contract for a staff job on a series would be for a limited time, maybe 8 weeks or 8 episodes. How do you "wow" them enough to bring you back? How does one go from the 8-week trial to being signed on for the rest of the year? Do you get a raise if they sign you on for the rest of the year?

Okay, to start out, your initial time period will be limited, yes. Not counted by episodes, though. Because you are a Staff Writer, your pay is a weekly pay, with a minimum set by the WGA depending on the amount of your initial employment. In other words, if it is 8 weeks, you get paid a certain amount (check the WGA website for the current rates). If it is 20 weeks, it's another amount, actually less per week than the 8 week rate. This is to encourage the company to employ you longer. Obviously you'd still want the 20 week deal because you will make more money overall. If you are a brand new Writer; if this is your first ever staff job, there is a baby-Writer rate as well. Which is less than the normal rates for your initial employment but jumps up to established rates once past the trial period.

If you are picked up on your option to extend your contract, yes, your rates will generally go up (for equivalent deals; comparing 20 weeks with a pickup for another 20 weeks). That's a staple in the business. For every option that is picked up, you get a little bit more. When I started, lo those many years ago, I believe I started with a ten week, then another ten week, then 22 weeks and, after that, a 52 week (the days of the 52 week deals are long gone). The key, of course, is to get that second option term picked up.

Honestly, from my experience, you really have to screw up to lose your first option pick up. Most people know and understand that this is your first shot. They will guide you. They don't expect you to know the business intuitively, so they will cut you some slack as long as you are able to rise to the occasion and do your part. Follow the guide of the Producers. If you ever have a question, ask. Just be interactive and alert. Stay up on things and be ready to get involved.

For that kind of money and commitment, you expect to be working day and night. Perhaps. When I started on staff, I went crazy because I expected to be in the middle of this hive of activity. But, at that level, you really aren't in it as much as you would think or might want. In fact, a lot of time is spent waiting for your next assignment, attending meetings and watching the Producers running around. So I was constantly worried that I wasn't doing enough to keep my job, when in fact, I was doing exactly what I was supposed to do. Don't obsess too much about it. Spend your down time working on story ideas. The Producers I started out with on *Riptide* were very interested in teaching me the business, so I was expected to attend editing sessions, music spotting and the like. As Tom Blomquist, the Producer for *Riptide* told me, "Think of this as Grad School. Except we're going to pay you to learn." It was to the advantage of the series to teach me the ropes. But, even then, I still had a lot of down time that drove me crazy.

By the same token, do NOT get swayed by the slow nature of your job. I had a Writer once who felt that it meant he could saunter in to the office when he wanted to or take a day off whenever he felt like it. I gave him every shot at redemption, I picked up his option three times, but I finally had to let him go. For the money you get paid, you can afford to be in your office on time if I require it. Not always because you know you have something to do, but because you never know when I (the Producer) will want you to do something. And if I say "Get Jimbo in here for a meeting" I don't want to hear that Jimbo decided not to come in today. And, by the way, if you notice the Producers sauntering in when they want to, keep in mind that you aren't a Producer. When you are, you'll find the rules will change for you. Until then, stay professional.

I made a LOT of mistakes when on my first job because I wasn't just ignorant about what staff jobs were, I was ignorant about the whole writing gig. I was self-taught, so I never had a chance to learn what was right or wrong as a Freelancer, much less as a Staff Writer. I learned all that later. But some of the mistakes I made back then were laughable.

Fortunately, I was working for people who had a sense of humor.

Then my partner and I were asked to rewrite a script. We did a horrible rewrite (hey, we had never done that sort of thing). The Producers knew we were new, obviously, but they wanted to give us something to do. I didn't know until years later that one of the Producers told the Exec Producer that they should can us. Fortunately, the Exec felt otherwise. She saw potential in us and knew that we needed some experience under our belt.

There was another time when we were trying to put out a first draft for the Producers to read. The operating procedure in this company was to write your draft, give it to the assistant who would take it to the copying room to make copies for the Producers to read. Then the notes and second draft and so on.

Well, just by the luck of the gods, we had a secretary who had never worked in Television or Film before. When we finished the script, we copied the style of title pages from another script from the previous year. We put the series name, title name, our names, date and F.R. after the date. We figured F.R. meant For Review. Well, it didn't. Turned out that it meant Full Run. Which means 200+ copies to be distributed to the cast, crew, studio, network, etc. Major "Oops!" Thank GOD someone caught it before it got out of the building. It was embarrassing!

Where were we? Oh, yes. Getting your option picked up. Or, rather, losing it. Another way you can lose your pickup is if the company has to cut back. This does happen as your pay goes up whenever your options are picked up. The company may decide it's cheaper to not have you on staff, but just give you freelance script assignments. So they might cut you and go on that plan.

There are many reasons why you might lose your job. If it has nothing to do with your creativity and is only a budget thing, the Producers will still find a way to work with you. But keep in mind how tenuous your job can be. Don't give a reason for them to cut you.

If a writer on a trial period is released (fired), will the company go out and bring another writer in to replace him on another trial basis?

It comes down to budget and need.

Let's say I have allocated money in my budget for two Staff Writers. I hire two Writers, both on 8 week options. One of them works out, one doesn't. I'm not going to hire a third Writer until I can free up that money. So I'll wait until the option expires on the bad Writer and let him go. Then I'll either hire a new Staff Writer, start a search for a replacement, or consider whether I need another Writer or not. It's possible that I might not. That would free the money up for other uses. But I would wait until the option has expired before hiring anyone else.

In general, there is no release of a Writer "during" the option period. In fact, it's not called a release, it's called "not picking up the option." In very rare cases, you will hear about a Writer being released, but not often at that level. The reason for that is because even if the company decides to let the Writer go, the company is still liable for the money. So the money, one way or another, is still gone. You will hear more often about Showrunners or Producers being let go and settlements made on their remaining contracts. This is usually for creative differences or political reasons. But at the level of Staff Writer, since the money is lost either way, the logic is to let you stay and run out your contract. You'd really have to be offensive to be barred from the office.

How long can I expect my career to last?

You're not going to like this. No one does. It's a hard question to answer because it depends on so many variables. But, in general, someone who breaks in as a Television Writer doesn't have a long career. Many people come and go quickly. They break in and can't make anything more of it. They get one staff job and it burns them out. It can be anything. Keep in mind, this is a difficult business to get into and even harder to stay in. And the vast majority of it is being unemployed, trying to get your next gig.

Here are a couple of unsettling facts. First, the older you get, the less they want you. Harsh. But it's true. Television is considered a "young" business and, often, the executives you meet are relatively young. There is a misconception that older Writers can't write younger characters. Although there's no apparent problem with believing younger Writers can write older characters. Truth is, a good Writer can write any age. But, again, it's not about ability, it's about perception.

Another fact is that the more you do work, the longer your resumé becomes, the harder it is for you to get work. You'd think it would be the exact opposite as the long term experience must have a value. But, no, your credits start to date you. They might start to think you're the person who writes that "old stuff." Not the current, hip material they need now.

If you're young and you're reading this thinking, hey, it doesn't apply to you, think again. You *are* going to get older. And, if you're lucky, you *are* going to have a resumé that dates you. Understand it now so it doesn't slap you later.

How to deal with this? Part of it is that, though your body might deteriorate with time, your mind and energy has to stay up there. You want to project that energy that gives the executives and Producers confidence in you. Keep your enthusiasm and optimism in your creativity. Do not, and this is important, do *not* let the natural cynicism or bitterness of this business get to you. Because it can get so frustrating, many Writers start to let their feelings show through. Don't do that.

As far as your credits are concerned, it's a problem in the world of the internet. It's very hard to hide your credits. Some Writers I know start to remove the older credits from their resumé and hope no one researches it. Others have even changed their name on their scripts in the hopes that a completely untraceable name has a better chance than the credit burdened name. For me, I never bothered to do either of those. I'm actually quite proud of my credits, so I leave them as they are.

Truthfully this only becomes a problem if there's a gap in your work. If, for example, you've been working steady for years then have a slow spell of a few months or a couple of years. If you have been working steadily and have a current show, no one really looks at the length of your credits. As they say, you're only as good as your last show.

Another thing every Television Writer should do is to *not* remain just a Writer. Your goal is to get on staff and move up through the ranks. You prolong your career if you become known as not just a Writer but as a Producer. That puts you in another category and enhances your chance of staying in for the long term.

And one final thing I have to mention. Learn how to save money. Seriously. Start a smart retirement plan early in your life and stick to it. Yes, the WGA has a great retirement plan if you can stay in long enough to be vested, but you're going to need more. Save money, invest smartly, and plan for the future. As I've said, the majority of this business is unemployment and you never know how long that will last. Or if it will ever end. It doesn't mean you can't live life or enjoy the money you're making. Just be smart.

Parental Advice Mode: Off.

XII. ODDS AND ENDS

Are there any shortcuts?

As newbies, you are anxious to get in. Anxious to get started and looking for any shortcut that will help you accomplish that. You are quick to listen when people know "secrets" to breaking in and you are willing to try things that seem unusual because, hey, this is an unusual business. That makes you … sheep. By that I mean that it makes you a target for scams and con artists. I cannot stress this enough. People sacrifice their sense of disbelief and listen to anyone who tells them what they want to hear. Consequently these people lose a lot of money and dignity while wasting time and learning the wrong lessons. Read carefully what I am about to write:

There. Are. No. Shortcuts.

Go back and read it again. And again. And when someone tells you they have one, remember what I said. There might be many different ways to accomplish your goal and avenues you can try. You doing one might be quicker than your neighbor doing the same thing. Me breaking into the business was considered short, but I know others who have been hitting their head against the wall for years doing the same thing. Was mine a "shortcut?"

The moment you start looking for shortcuts is the moment that the con artists say "gotcha!"

Branding Yourself

This is really under the heading of "Marketing Yourself." As I mentioned earlier, when you break into the Television business, you will probably be pigeon-holed by your first success. If you are known as an action writer, it will be hard for others to consider you as a romance writer. Now, that's not necessarily a bad thing. If there are a lot of action series, you'll do well. Ride that wave as long as you can. But what usually happens is the Writer starts getting bored with the work he's getting. He wants to spread his wings, try something new, prove himself in another arena. But no one will give him that shot. No matter how great that coming-of-age romance drama screenplay is that you wrote, no one is really interested. You are the primo action Writer and that's what they want. Frustrating. But, again, not a bad thing as far as a career is concerned. Your work has "branded" you as a particular type of Writer.

There is another kind of branding, though. And that's the overall impression you give to people and how they know you. It's your look, your style, the vibe you give off, it's many things that make up your "presence" to others.

Confused? Yeah, it's a strange one. So I have to use myself as an example. My branding is my hat. Yes. That's it. For some reason, I have a face that naturally goes with my fedora. I originally bought the hat to keep the sun off my pasty-white scalp through my thinning hair, but now I am so identified with my hat that if I don't wear it, its absence becomes the conversation. I have been referred to many times as "the guy with the hat." In fact, I have auctioned off my retired hats for charity. True.

Aside from the fact that it goes against my basic Southern upbringing to constantly wear a hat, especially indoors, I've gotten used to it. It's part of how the business knows me. Now I'm not recommending that you go out and buy a fedora and try to brand yourself, but you should be aware that this is going to happen. And you need to understand how that branding affects your business prospects. You're going to be known for something aside from your work. Embrace it and, if you can, utilize it.

In other words, keep in mind that, in Television, your writing talent isn't all they are buying. They are buying you; you are a product. Products can gain or lose value by mere perception.

On a related note, and being very blunt, if you don't keep up your hygiene and have constant bad breath, guess what your branding will be? But if you dress well in a particular style with a particular demeanor, it will be noted and you will be remembered for it.

So much of what people remember about meeting someone isn't what was said or discussed, it was the "feel" they had when they walked away. Just like one of your characters, you want your audience to immediately identify things about you when they first interact with you.

Just remember it.

Your Name

This almost sounds silly mentioning, but in this business, your name is your calling card. It has value. It's the reason why we fight so much over credits. It's the most common thing people associate with your work so make sure you get it out there as much as possible in the right manner. And don't feel petty about insisting it's spelled correctly.

Case in point, with me again. My Writing name is Steven L. Sears. Not Steve Sears, not Steven Sears. But you'd be surprised how many times I've had to clarify that to people who are putting my name in print. In their mind, they think that I'm just being petty. Why would a couple of letters be so important? For the same reason any company or corporation wants to make sure their names are correctly spelled, you need to do the same.

Your name is your business. It's how people will search for you. It's how they associate you with your work. And, more importantly, your name will be a WGA registered name. Everything from credits to payments will be determined on it. I can promise you, Steve Sears would love to get some of my residuals. And he would fight to make sure his name was just as protected as I protect mine.

Oh, and get it on a business card. Always carry your cards with you. *Always.*

How do you tell the difference between a con artist and someone who is really trying to help?

Remember the chapter on the possibility of a Producer conning you? This is more of the same. Expanded a bit and important enough to discuss again.

Con artists are good at what they do, and what they do is fool you into thinking you're getting something you're not. In this business, it's a matter of making you believe someone can fulfill your dreams. So I can list a few things to be careful of, but they are by far not all of them. And they are things that a good Con Artist will have answers for if challenged.

And I don't just include people who deceive you for money. There are those who just get a power rush by convincing people they know what they are talking about. Others who try to sabotage other's success because of their lack of it. But let's deal with the Con Artist in the traditional sense.

A Con Artist wants something from you, whether it's cash or a script or something of a more amorous arrangement or something. The Con Artist will offer something in exchange for this and make it seem as if you are getting a bargain and that what they are offering is standard operating procedure in the business. They will couch the exchange in very reasonable and attractive terms. The bottom line is to look at, well, the bottom line. If you are giving something to someone, you are potentially being scammed. You have to look at the value of what you get in return. More importantly, you have to be able to assess the validity of what you are receiving.

You can easily ask around to people who are in the business or have some experience in the business for advice. Yes, you'll hear many different opinions, but with all that, you'll be better able to discern the value of the advice. If it all checks out, you should be prepared to actually act on the advice. I am constantly amazed at how many people have asked my advice on situations that were obvious cons. Yet, even when I have pointed out how they are being ripped off, they have insisted that this situation is different. These kind of people are the people that con artists love. Not only have they bought the bill of goods, they are now defending it. Don't be one of those people. Use your head.

I will tell you one thing as an absolute truth. If you decide to enter this business, someone will try to scam you. You will be tempted. If you're lucky, you'll feel a little tingle in your gut that tells you something just isn't right. If you're smart, you'll listen to your gut and walk away. *Never* be afraid to walk away.

What about managers?

Managers … a much discussed topic. Right up front, I'll tell you that the right Manager is valuable. There are some great ones out there. But there are very very few good Managers who can do anyone any good.

Keep this in mind: Anyone can print up a card and say they are a Manager. There is no regulation. Agents, at least, are franchised by the WGA. And the ones that aren't are easy to question by using the standards set by the WGA. No such case with the title of Manager.

To illustrate, here is a post from a new Writer online:

> *"I wrote a screenplay and got a manager and he is connected in Hollywood. He knows most of the top people and says he's gonna get my screenplay sold."*

If you examine this, there is nothing that gives any validity to this person claiming to be a Manager. Upon questioning, this person admitted he knew nothing about the Manager except what the Manager claimed. The assumptions of Hollywood connections was based entirely on what the Manager claimed. There was no proof of it and no guarantee of anything. But, as if this wasn't bad enough, the message goes on:

> *"The contract he wants me to sign gives him half of the money as his share and a producing job on the film, but it is only for this first script. I have been trying to get a manager or Agent for two months and don't think anyone else will be as interested or be as motivated as someone who stands to make half. I think this is the greatest motivator because money is at the root of all work. If he can sell my second screenplay, I'd be happy to give him half again."*

This is outrageous. And it is exactly what I am talking about. This person is so anxious to break in that they have thrown their common sense to the wayside. Even worse, this person is willing to sign a contract for this "service."

Here's what I wrote in response:

> *"This is a mistake on so many levels.*
>
> *Any manager who asks for half YOUR money is a scam artist with no credibility in the industry. I can say that without even knowing the person. This is a person who is talking a big talk because he knows you want to hear it. He knows what to say to get you excited. He will even get you excited about carrying the upfront financial burden for the effort (has he mentioned "office costs" for "postage" or "filing" or anything like that? He will and will expect you*

to pay for it. And, no, you shouldn't pay for any of it).

I know that as you are starting out, you are eager to make that first sale and will react to anything that seems "legit." But at this point, you don't really know what is right or wrong in the business. You don't really know the business at all. But because of your eagerness, you are prime territory for con men. I don't say this to make you feel bad, believe me. This is something we have all gone through at one time or another.

Managers are strange creatures, even when they are legit and do what they are supposed to do. But Managers are not regulated by any authority except normal state business law. You may think that's enough, it isn't. It means that anyone can say they are a Manager and sign you to any kind of contract they want, taking huge advantages over you and your work that, in the real Hollywood Industry, would have your "Manager" thrown out of the lowest industry bar in the city. Legitimate Agents franchise with the WGA by agreeing to standards and rules designed to protect writers from being taken advantage of.

Managers don't have those restrictions. They can sign you to anything they please and you are bound by the legal strength of that contract, no matter what rights you sell away just to get "a chance." Put it this way: The WGA franchise is designed to protect the Writer. The State Law is designed to protect the contract.

As if what I've said isn't hard enough to take, I have to add more. And, again, this isn't directed toward you, but toward the situation you are in, which is one that many will find themselves in. Because anyone can be a Manager, the only Managers who MIGHT be any good are the ones who have a track record. And those people (as strange as this sounds) aren't looking for new people. Certainly not new people from outside of Los Angeles. They are looking for established Writers who have credits that they can easily sell.

Ideally you want that rarest of creatures: A successful Manager who is on the lookout for the next big breakout success, someone the Manager can have confidence in and go to the mat for. If you find one, let me know. I have yet to. And I can absolutely guarantee you, this "Manager" of yours is not that person.

Managers do, by the way, try to attach their names to projects as producers. It's something that is ridiculous, but it isn't uncommon.

Now, you might ask, why NOT go ahead and sign with this "Manager" on the off, rare chance that he might actually do something?

The contract that you sign can have anything in it, anything. And you will be bound by that contract for its life. And, a bit of the life afterward.

For example: Let's say that you sign a three year contract. The manager does nothing for you. In fact, you discover that the manager has several newbie writers and scripts which he has signed and, same as you, he is doing nothing for them. He's playing the odds. It costs him nothing and on the off chance that YOU happen to sell your script (without his help), you are STILL bound by that contract.

Why would he do such a thing? He knows that your eagerness/desperation/frustration is going to make you move on something no matter what he does or doesn't do. Even if you confront him and tell him off, he won't care. He has a contract.

Then, if you manage to finish out your three year contract and sell your script after the contract expires ... you now have a lawsuit. He can claim that his assistance and connections led to your eventual sale, proving to the court that his assistance was invaluable and a necessary part to the success of the sale.

By the way ... everything I've written above isn't the rare, worst case scenario. It happens.

You have three things working against you.

1. Your eagerness for something to happen with your script. You are willing to suspend disbelief in order to have a shot at it. The most logical thinking person in the world does this in these scenarios. Yet that same person would walk out of, say, [a] hardware store or car dealership if the equivalent promises were made.

2. Your inexperience with the business and the way things are done. This does, obviously, take experience. You can't be faulted for not having it (actually you can't be faulted for any of this). You are smart in asking for advice. It's up to you how you react to it, though.

3. Something that is common to even experienced pros; you are afraid to confront and demand answers. You are so afraid that you will scare this guy off that you haven't demanded proof of his claims. You have EVERY RIGHT to ask him for a list of his successes and the people you can contact to verify his claims. You have EVERY RIGHT to walk back in with your OWN contract and tell him that this is the only thing you will sign. You, in fact, have ALL the rights here: it's YOUR script you are talking about. Demand answers and DO NOT accept the answers he gives you without verifying.

He will give you excuses; he will tell you he can't divulge that information for legal reasons; he will get upset and tell you that he can't work with someone who doesn't have faith in him; he will do what he has to do to deflect your question. Don't buy any of it, this is a business and you have every right to ask and demand.

So what should you expect a manager to get for his services?

Legitimate Managers will take only five to fifteen percent of your income AFTER you have been paid by the studio.

That's it. Go back to your "manager" and tell him that you want a 10% deal with a limited one year contract. Watch the fur fly when he hears that. And be prepared for his "outrage" [at] your insolence! Then, when he calms down a bit, tell him the following:

You will NOT pay him ANYTHING upfront. If he needs copies of your script, YOU will go out and make them then give him the copies. Do NOT rely on him to make copies.

Postage, filing fees, office fees, all of this is HIS overhead, not yours.

Your contract is of a limited time and with well defined rules. I would suggest that you get an attorney to look over the contract and explain everything (and, no, don't use the manager's attorney). The money is well worth it. An entertainment attorney is best.

You will expect and demand to be kept up with his efforts, who he is contacting and what the results of the contacts here. You should know everywhere your script is being sent. The non-legit manager will tell you not to worry about that. This is your career; you can bet you need to know who is seeing your material.

And, most important, you will walk out the door if you don't get your way. He will tell you you are being unreasonable. I will tell you right now that NONE of those demands are unreasonable and, in fact, are considered the basics of the manager/client relationship in the Industry.

I doubt there is anything this "manager" will do that you couldn't do own your own. You can get a list of agents or studios or development people and you can make blind phone calls and submissions on your own. That is the most that this guy is going to do for you. He isn't even allowed to negotiate a contract for you, that's the realm of your attorney or Agent.

There are a few good ones out there. This person you are talking to isn't one of them, quite the opposite. And I'm telling you right now, having NO manager is better than having the WRONG one."

I'm happy to report that the person who posted the questions reconsidered his association with this "manager." I give him credit for asking the question and, more importantly, putting his immediate desires aside long enough to consider the answer. Even when, I have to admit, my reply was very direct and blunt.

What if a producer asks be to write a script for free? Isn't that worth it?

This can be subtle, this can be direct. Someone may give you a line about how they can get your script produced, but you'll get paid after the movie is sold. Or (something that I was approached with) someone might "suggest" that you write a script and that they will guide you and give you input for free. All they ask is the first rights to the script. It's still writing for free with no guarantee of payment.

So the answer is no. Absolutely not. A legitimate Producer wouldn't dare ask you to do that. First of all, it is prohibited by the WGA contracts. Secondly, it shows their regard for your talent and ability.

You are the one to set your self-worth. If you think it's zero, then that's what others will think. And, even if you did do this, what does it mean to your career? It means that you are the best free Writer around. And others will approach you on that level.

This is a problem usually found in the Feature world and not so much in Television, though it isn't unknown.

What about Internet screenwriting boards or chat rooms? Are they helpful?

Yes ... and no. This is something that I have become quite familiar with. At the beginning of this book, I mentioned that I wrote this because I was being asked a lot of questions about screenwriting. By far, the vast majority of those questions came through the internet. People on boards would ask a question and I would answer them if I could. But the internet is like running around in a maze of doors, trying to find the bathroom. You desperately want to find what you are looking for, but you don't want to try every door to get there. The information you get on these boards can be great if you know how to read them. But a lot of it is not only wrong, it's harmful.

For example, do you know that I don't know how to Write? Or that I don't understand the Business? Okay, okay, after reading this book, it might not be that much of a stretch. But I mean despite a three decade career of writing, I am apparently making "amateur" mistakes. Yes, there are people who have told me that. I can only get away with it, they say, because I'm successful. In other words, the industry cuts me some slack because I work. Of course, I have been writing scripts pretty much the same since I started, so I'm not sure when the slack started to get cut in my direction.

Confused? Me, too. I'll try to explain. When you go to these boards, you have to understand a few things. First of all, you are an aspiring Writer, but almost everyone else there is as well. Some may have a few scripts written, some have none at all. All of them will talk about the idea/script they have under consideration with a major studio/Director/Actor, etc. Most of this is all hype or tenuous truth at best. These people (for the most part) are just about where you are, except they've been on the particular board longer.

Now, despite the fact that they are no farther along than you are, many of them consider themselves to be authorities on screenwriting and the business because they have A: read a lot of books; B: listened to a lot of professionals talk about it; or, C: heard about the rules from the internet. It's this last part that's the problem. The "rules." I'm not sure where they started, but according to these boards, there are "rules" you have to follow in writing your screenplay. And if you don't follow these "rules," you are an amateur and will be laughed out of the business. No, actually you will never be laughed out of the business because no one will take you seriously enough to allow you in to the business in the first place.

Whoa, sounds scary. It would make sense to get a list of some of these "rules" and follow them to the letter. Well, here are a few of the ones dealing with script format:

1. Never use the phrase "we see" in a script.

2. Never use CAPS.

3. Never use Transitions.

4. Never call a camera angle.

5. Never use three brads in the binding.

6. Never be descriptive in your action. Just write the basics.

7. Never write parentheticals for the characters.

Seems easy enough to follow, doesn't it? And there are reasons why they will say these are "rules." For example:

1. Why say "we see?" Isn't it obvious? We are "seeing" the screenplay on the screen, so saying "we see" is redundant.

2. Using CAPS is old school. It interrupts the flow.

3. Why use "CUT TO"? It's implied when you change scenes. And what's the difference between "CUT TO" and "SMASH CUT TO"?

4. If you call an angle, you'll insult the Director. It's his job, not yours.

5. Two brads is the rule.

6. Putting too much description isn't necessary.

The set designer will handle the set, the Actors will handle movement and characterization, the Director will handle the mood.

7. Actors hate parentheticals because they don't like to be told how to give a line reading.

When you explain it that way, it certainly makes sense. Except....

1. You aren't seeing a screenplay, you are reading it. And the Writer's job is to write in such a way that the reader can envision the movie in their imagination. When you say "we see" you are giving them the perspective, the camera angle if you will, of what is in the scene. It helps them get a vision in their mind.

2. CAPS may be old school, but it is still used when a new character is introduced. Why? Because it allows the reader to put a mental stickpin into that character so that they aren't thumbing backwards to see if they have seen the character before. Remember, you aren't writing in a prose format where you can elaborate on the character at first meeting.

3. In TV, transitions are still used in most cases. They aren't so much used in screenplays. But they did (and do) serve a function. They put a stop point on the flow of a scene, both geographic as well as emotional. If I write two characters talking as they walk from a lobby into a hallway into an office as a continuous scene, I'll write those three locations without transitions. But if I then got to another part of town, where I have effectively stopped the flow of

the previous scene, I'll use a "CUT TO:" And as to the difference between a "CUT TO" and a "SMASH CUT TO" it has to do with the timing of a scene for impact. If it's just a "CUT TO," the editor will let the scene play out, hanging on the last character a bit. If it's a "SMASH CUT TO," the Editor knows to truncate the scene in order to go to the next scene quickly, thus giving it more of an impact.

4. If you call every angle, yeah, it's a bit bothersome to everyone. But there are times when you, as the Writer, want to point out something exceptional as a part of the scene. Foreshadowing or subtext or something. Calling an ANGLE on something like that isn't just okay, it might be necessary.

5. If you send me a script with three brads, I might pull the middle one out and save it for my own use, but I'm not going to send the script back because of it.

6. If you follow the rule of putting only the essential information in, your script will become antiseptic and sterile. It won't be a fun read. When I write, I like to layer what I say in my action so that I not only describe what I need in the location, but I set a mood as well. Saying that there is "a typewriter on a desk" tells me nothing about the character who owns it. But "an old Royal typewriter, the key letters almost erased from use, sits on the cracked mahogany desk …" tells me a lot about the character and what he is like. For me, this is necessary information since

I don't want to waste time saying it in dialogue.

7. Actors do hate parentheticals and precisely for that reason. However, there are times when a line can be interpreted many different ways. In those occasions, it's best that you indicate the manner so that the line fits into the context of the scene.

O   O   O

Now, with what I just wrote about "rules," don't start thinking that I have just given you the absolute "anti-rules." Or that I have given you the complete run-down of "rules" you're going to hear out there. Nitpicky things that, you are told, you must follow without question or your career is over before it starts.

What I am trying to say is that there is a time a place for all those things. And, more importantly, used correctly it's not going to destroy your career. I have done every one of these things and never had a problem. Most of the professionals I've worked with have pretty much the same experience. Yet these people on the boards will preach this as if it's a Gospel. And Heaven forbid you might violate the sanctity of the "rules."

Now the amusing thing for me is that when I tell people that these "rules" are, at best, guidelines and not absolute, I get told that I'm wrong. I'm not trying to toot my horn here, but I have been doing this for a while. I just might know what I am talking about.

The question is, how are you supposed to know the difference? If "A" says one thing and "B" says the opposite, which is the truth? Well that's why a lot of research is required. Not just on the question, but on the people answering you. If "A" is a working Writer and "B" is an aspirant ... well, I think you see the difference.

Now, even saying that, keep in mind that we professionals disagree on the finer points as well. That's why you do research, asking the same question many places to find an answer. But usually, if it's a question on script format, the answer is easy to find. Read screenplays and teleplays. Produced screenplays and teleplays. You'll begin to see consistencies among the scripts and, at the same time, you'll see differences. For the most part, the consistencies can be taken as "rules" and the differences can be taken as guidelines.

But how do you know the pros from the amateurs? This isn't the easiest thing to do. Asking for someone's credits is frowned upon on these boards. For good reason, actually. For one thing, those people without credits don't want to feel that their opinions don't count. Also, those people with credits might not want others to know that because they don't want people trying to use them; asking them to read scripts or introduce them to agents and the like. Still others don't like to talk about their credits because it comes off as bragging. I fall into the latter category, but I do have a rule. If someone asks me, I'll tell them. If they don't, I don't.

Now the next thing you might notice in the room

is the, shall we say, bluntness of the room. The internet offers a certain amount of anonymous protection that makes lions out of lambs. It's a new interactive dynamic that throws the normal social cues on their side. In other words, people are more likely to be rude and insulting. What can you do about that? Well, that's up to you, but I personally don't think it's worth getting into a pissing contest on the internet. Take it for what it is, shrug it off and move on. Remember that these people don't know you either. They will have no effect on anything in your life unless you let them.

Having said that, I've certainly gotten into a few "heated" discussions. At a certain point, I have to admit to a perverse enjoyment. I will just tell the person that I'm no longer debating more than I am "sport fishing." That's my way of saying "this is no longer a discussion."

Okay, I've made the internet scene sound pretty bleak and scary. I mean, why would anyone want to get involved with it? Well, I just gave you the bad side. The good side is overwhelmingly helpful. There are a lot of people who are truly interested in screenwriting and learning about it. Many of them will form local Writer's groups to get together and discuss scripts. Many more will maintain contact with you and become part of your network. And there are a lot of professionals who feel the need to give back with their knowledge and experience. If you ask a question you will get an answer. As long as you are respectful to the people in the room and show a true desire to learn. Of all the things that the internet has brought for the Writer's use, this networking is in the top two things of importance (the other being instant research on almost any subject).

And … you can order pizza online. To a working Writer, this is Nirvana.

Is there a casting couch for writers?

This question might surprise many. For Actors and Actresses, well, it's a given that it happens. But for Writers???

Sadly, there is. Face it, there is a "couch" for any job that people crave. Now I'm not going to moralize here (anyone who knows me personally knows I have no right to do that), but put things in perspective. If you meet someone and they knock your socks off, hey, do what feels right for two consenting adults. But doing it because you think it will help your career is a mistake. You'll be known for a different talent than Writing and when they pass your name around to their friends (and they will), that's the only kind of meetings you'll be getting.

If you are comfortable with that, then you'll have a fine time in Hollywood because there are a lot of people looking for you. But never think that you have to do it. I'll say it again, you have the right to walk away from anything that makes you uncomfortable.

And by doing it, you will define yourself to others.

Whether or not you sleep with others isn't as important as whether you can sleep with yourself at night. Your self-respect is irreplaceable. No one can take it away, you can only give it away.

XIII. Final Words

Zymotically.
Zymurgy.
Zythum.

At least according to my Webster's New Twentieth Century Unabridged Dictionary of the English Language.

As for me, I have little to say in conclusion. When people ask me what's it like to be a Writer, I say that it is the most debilitating, frustrating, wearying, maddening, illogical thing I have ever tried to do.

And by far the most rewarding.

I wish you luck.

ABOUT THE AUTHOR

Steven L. Sears has been a Staff Writer, Story Editor and Producer on such shows as *Stingray, The A-Team, JJ Starbuck, The Highwayman, Father Dowling Mysteries, Swamp Thing,* and *Raven.* In addition, he has written for shows such as *Hardcastle & McCormick, Superboy, The Hollywood Detective, Jesse Hawkes, Hardball, Grandslam, Walker–Texas Ranger,* and many others, as well as developing Television Pilots, Features, Interactive and animation for several studios and networks. He was Co-Executive Producer of the hit syndicated series *Xena: Warrior Princess,* and the Co-Creator and Executive Producer of the Columbia/TriStar Television Series *Sheena.* Stepping outside the world of Film and Television, Steven co-authored the novel series *VilleAnne* with author Peter J. Wacks and co-created and co-authored the graphic novel *Stalag-X* with *Times* Bestselling author Kevin J. Anderson.

THE MILLION DOLLAR WRITING SERIES

Drawing on the Power of Resonance in Writing

Million Dollar Book Signings

Million Dollar Outlines

Million Dollar Productivity

Million Dollar Professionalism

The Non-User-Friendly Guide for Aspiring TV Writers